THEY
FOUND
*the*SECRET

THEY FOUND *the* SECRET

*20 Transformed Lives
That Reveal
a Touch of Eternity*

V. RAYMOND EDMAN

ZondervanPublishingHouse
Grand Rapids, Michigan

A Division of HarperCollins*Publishers*

They Found the Secret
Copyright © 1960, 1984 by The Zondervan Corporation

Requests for information should be addressed to:

📖 ZondervanPublishingHouse
Grand Rapids, Michigan 49530

Library of Congress Cataloging-in-Publication Data

Edman, V. Raymond (Victor Raymond), 1900–1967.
    They found the secret
        p.   cm.
    (Clarion classic)
    Bibliography: p.
    1. Converts—Biography.   2. Christian biography.
BV4930.E3   1983   209'.2'2[B]   83–23576
ISBN: 0-310-24051-4

Interior design by Jody DeNeef

Printed in the United States of America

98 99 00 01 02 03 04/❖ DC/ 10 9 8 7 6 5 4 3 2 1

Contents

Victor Raymond Edman

𝒱ictor Raymond Edman, best remembered as the fourth president of Wheaton College (Ill.) and writer of many devotional books, was born in Chicago Heights in 1900. He served in the Army Medical Corps during World War I where he learned to appreciate history, to practice simple medicine, which later would be of great use to him on the mission field, and to trust God completely. Through some difficult times he was brought to the realization that only total abandonment to God could lead to experiencing God's fullest blessing. After the war, Edman studied at the University of Illinois, Nyack Missionary Training Institute (NY) and Boston University, from which he graduated in 1923.

Edman served as a missionary to Ecuador from 1923 to 1928, during which time he preached, traveled, counseled, and served as an educator. In 1925 he nearly died from a tropical disease. The experience was one that profoundly affected him for the rest of his life. It was during a time of unconsciousness, while all were awaiting his death, and his wife having made all the funeral arrangements, that he experienced the overwhelming presence of God. Feeling himself lifted above that scene and into the glorious presence of God he desired nothing more than to ascend forever. However, he heard a quiet voice telling him to return, and a slow descent began, which resulted in his regaining consciousness and recovering from his illness. Unknown to him prayer meetings were being held, at that very time, back in the United States for him. From

that moment on, although often called upon to suffer physi-
cally and emotionally, Edman's life was characterized by a
sense of God's presence and never failing good cheer. He had
seen beyond the veil, and what had greeted him was the
unfathomable love of God, an ultimate beyond which one
need not go, in this life or the next.

He earned a Ph.D. in International Relations from Clark
University in 1933, then taught at Nyack Missionary Training
Institute for a year, before going to Wheaton College, where he
taught Political Science from 1936–1940. He became the president of Wheaton College in 1940 and remained so until 1965
when he retired to become Chancellor, a largely honorary post.
He died while speaking in chapel on September 22, 1967.

Edman's deep devotional life expressed itself in everything
he did. He was unfailingly cheerful, even in the face of deep
discouragement or pain, both of which he knew from prolonged personal experience. One acquaintance said of him,
"He is the most giving man I know, I mean of himself. It has
always amazed me that such a busy and well-known man
would take time out to drop me a few lines and to always
remember me at Christmas with a gift of his latest book. He
truly was Christlike in his interest and compassion for others."
He was also able to write about his devotional life in such a
way that others were neither offended by the personal revela-
tions made, nor drawn unduly to him, but rather pointed to
the Lord. Not many devotional writers have been able to do
this very successfully.

Two of Dr. Edman's books stand out as being of greatest
significance, judging from reviews and comments written to
him over the years, *The Disciplines of Life* and *They Found the
Secret*. *They Found the Secret* began as a series of twenty articles
written for *Christian Life* magazine that were gathered together
in book form in 1960. What Edman tried to do was to show in

the actual lives of Christian people how the power of Christ, called by him "the indwelling life of Christ," was the source of every believer's spiritual strength. This had been a much neglected theme in the writings of evangelical Christians for the last fifty years or so. Dr. Edman's goal was to put the idea into the mainstream of the movement so that all could benefit by entering into a life-transforming relationship with Christ. It is not enough just to know about Christ, or to know about what He did for us, nor even to experience His work in us. What is needed is to experience *Him* in us, as He works out God's inscrutable will. Students of mysticism and spirituality will recognize this immediately as being in the tradition of mystical union, although, in this case, given a twentieth-century protestant interpretation.

One of Dr. Edman's favorite phrases was "not somehow—but triumphantly." This characterized his life as well as the lives of those written about in *They Found the Secret*. It can characterize our lives, too, if we listen carefully and open ourselves up to the work of Christ in us, as they did.

WALTER ELWELL
Wheaton College
Wheaton, Illinois

Introduction

Every now and then we come across a life that is radiant, revealing a richness, a warmth, a triumph that intrigues and challenges us.

These lives we find in biographies out of the past: and just when we begin to think that such people lived only in other days we meet one in real life, right in the middle of the twentieth century!

The details of their experiences are usually quite different; yet as we listen to their stories and watch their lives, either in our reading or in our contact with them, we begin to see a pattern that reveals their secret. Out of discouragement and defeat they have come into victory. Out of weakness and weariness they have been made strong. Out of ineffectiveness and apparent uselessness they have become efficient and enthusiastic.

The pattern seems to be self-centeredness, self-effort, increasing inner dissatisfaction and outer discouragement, a temptation to give it all up because there is no better way, and then finding the Spirit of God to be their strength, their guide, their confidence and companion—in a word, their life.

The crisis of the deeper life is the key that unlocks the secret of their transformation. It is the beginning of the *exchanged life*.

What is the exchanged life? Really, it is not some *thing*; it is some *One*. It is the indwelling of the Lord Jesus Christ made real and rewarding by the Holy Spirit.

There is no more glorious reality in all the world. It is life with a capital *L*.

It is new life for old. It is rejoicing for weariness and radiance for dreariness. It is strength for weakness and steadiness for uncertainty. It is triumph even through tears and tenderness of heart instead of touchiness. It is lowliness of spirit instead of self-exaltation and loveliness of life because of the presence of the altogether Lovely One.

Adjectives can be multiplied to describe it: abundant, overflowing, overcoming, all-pervading, satisfying, joyous, victorious; and each is but one aspect of a life that can be experienced but not fully explained.

Said the Savior: "I am come that they might have life, and that they might have it more abundantly." We find newness of life in Christ by receiving Him as our own Savior from the penalty of sin. Abundance of that life we find by surrendering self and drawing on the unfailing resources of the Almighty. There is life and then there is life more abundant. This is the exchanged life.

The expression, "the exchanged life," was first used, as far as I know, by J. Hudson Taylor, founder of the China Inland Mission. Out of striving and struggling, out of discouragement and defeat he came to the realization of life more abundant in Christ. I have found no happier description than his: The Exchanged Life.

And I have found no more concise contrast between the old and the new than that stated by the late Dr. A. B. Simpson in his poem entitled *Himself*.

Once it was the blessing, now it is the Lord;
Once it was the feeling, now it is His Word;
Once His gifts I wanted, now the Giver own;
Once I sought for healing, now Himself alone.

Once 'twas painful trying, now 'tis perfect trust;
Once a half salvation, now the uttermost;
Once 'twas ceaseless holding, now He holds me fast;
Once 'twas constant drifting, now my anchor's cast.

Once 'twas busy planning, now 'tis trustful prayer;
Once 'twas anxious caring, now He has the care;
Once 'twas what I wanted, now what Jesus says;
Once 'twas constant asking, now 'tis ceaseless praise.

Once it was my working, His it hence shall be;
Once I tried to use Him, now He uses me;
Once the power I wanted, now the Mighty One;
Once for self I labored, now for Him alone....

In this book are testimonies of men and women who have found the promise of life more abundant to be true. With procedure proper to a witness they tell us what happened, rather than attempting to teach us in fine detail the doctrine of their experience. From a multitude of witnesses throughout the centuries I have chosen just a few by way of illustration. The pattern of their experiences is much the same. They had believed on the Savior, yet they were burdened and bewildered, unfaithful and unfruitful, always yearning for a better way and never achieving by their efforts a better life. Then they came to a crisis of utter heart surrender to the Savior, a meeting with Him in the innermost depths of their spirit; and they found the Holy Spirit to be an unfailing fountain of life and refreshment. Thereafter life was never again the same, because in one way or another they had learned what the apostle Paul had testified: "I am crucified with Christ; nevertheless I live; yet not I, but Christ liveth in me; and the life which I now live in the flesh I live by the faith of the Son of God, who loved me, and gave himself for me." New life had been exchanged for old.

I have deliberately chosen witnesses of diverse personalities and backgrounds. God is no respecter of persons! There are those of yesteryear like John Bunyan, and of today like Richard C. Halverson and William P. Nicholson. There are clergymen like A. J. Gordon, and laymen like Dwight L. Moody.

Some are well known, like Charles G. Finney, while others may be little known or even quite forgotten, like J. A. Wood. There are mystics like Andrew Murray and practical men like Charles G. Trumbull and Robert E. Nicholas. There are women as well as men: Frances Ridley Havergal of England, Amy Carmichael of India, and Eugenia Price of contemporary America.

The details of their experience of the crisis of the deeper life are delightfully different; yet their testimony to the reality of the joy and power of the Spirit-filled life is unanimous. Nowhere in Scripture are we taught to seek experience. Rather, the Word says, "Seek ye the Lord." It is He who satisfies the longing soul. He is the secret of the exchanged life!

Rowena Planck Carr helped in the preparation of the manuscript, and typing was done by Ella Erickson, Ruth E. Buck, Lenora Knauer, JoAnne Morris Smith and Alice Holmes. Ivy T. Olson, Carol Primmer, and the library staff of the college have sought diligently the source materials needed.

Robert Walker, editor of *Christian Life,* has graciously consented to the use of material that has appeared in that periodical. Other publishers have kindly granted permission to quote pertinent portions from biographies they have printed.

To each of these, my heartfelt thanks!

V. RAYMOND EDMAN
Wheaton, Illinois

Chapter One

J. HUDSON TAYLOR
The Exchanged Life

*H*e was a joyous man now, a bright, happy Christian. He had been a toiling, burdened one before, with latterly not much rest of soul. It was resting in Jesus now, and letting Him do the work—which makes all the difference!" Thus spoke a fellow missionary of Hudson Taylor.

The pioneer missionary in the interior of China who had come to full realization of the Savior as the ever-present, indwelling One, testified: "My soul is so happy in the Lord! And as I think of the blessing He gave me on the happy day . . . I know not how sufficiently to thank and praise Him. Truly Jesus is the great need of our souls. And He is the great gift of our Father's love—who gave himself *for* us, and makes us one *with* him in resurrection life and power."

The deep dealing of God with His children varies in detail but the general pattern seems much alike for individual cases. Into each life there arises an awareness of failure, a falling short of all that one should be in the Lord; then there is a definite meeting with the risen Savior in utter surrender of heart, which is indeed death to self. There follows an appropriation by faith of His resurrection life through the abiding presence of the Holy Spirit. As a result there is realized an overflow of life likened by the Lord Jesus to "rivers of water." (See John 7:37–39.)

As a lad Hudson Taylor had come to know the Lord Jesus as his personal Savior. In his youth he had been called to the

mission field of China. For fifteen years he had served earnestly and effectively in that land before he came into experiential
possession of "the exchanged life." At the age of thirty-seven he
opened his heart to his mother in a long letter that expressed
his innermost hunger and thirst:

"My own position becomes continually more and more
responsible, and my need greater of special grace to fill it; but
I have continually to mourn that I follow at such a distance and
learn so slowly to imitate my precious Master. I cannot tell you
how I am buffeted sometimes by temptation. I never knew
how bad a heart I had. Yet I do know that I love God and love
His work, and desire to serve Him only in all things. And I
value above all things that precious Savior in Whom alone I
can be accepted. Often I am tempted to think that one so full
of sin cannot be a child of God at all; but I try to throw it back,
and rejoice all the more in the preciousness of Jesus, and in the
riches of that grace that has made us 'accepted in the Beloved.'
Beloved He is of God; beloved He ought to be of us. But oh,
how short I fall here again! May God help me to love Him more
and serve Him better. Do pray for me. Pray that the Lord will
keep me from sin, will sanctify me wholly, will use me more
largely in His service."

The human heart has no desires that God cannot satisfy.
The Christian's greatest difficulty is to take literally the promises of the Savior. Said the Lord Jesus: "If any man thirst, let him
come unto me and drink." We are told to come to Him, not to
some friend, not to some experience, not to some feeling or
frame of mine. We are not even to come just to the Word of
God: rather, we are to go through that Word to the person of
the Lord Jesus Himself.

The way to heart satisfaction and rest of sprit for Hudson
Taylor was learned from a fellow missionary, John McCarthy. In
a letter to Mr. Taylor he wrote:

"To let my loving Savior work in me His will, my sanctification is what I would live for by His grace. Abiding, not striving nor struggling; looking off unto Him; trusting Him for present power; trusting Him to subdue all inward corruption;
resting in the love of an almighty Savior, in the conscious joy
of a complete salvation, a salvation 'from all sin' (this is His
Word); willing that His will should truly be supreme—this is
not new, and yet 'tis new to me. I feel as though the first dawning of a glorious day had risen upon me. I hail it with trembling, yet with trust. I seem to have got to the edge only, but of
a sea which is boundless; to have sipped only, but of that
which fully satisfies. Christ literally all seems to me now the
power, the only power for service; the only ground for
unchanging joy. May He lead us into the realization of His
unfathomable fullness."

The Lord used this letter literally to lead Mr. Taylor "into
the realization of His unfathomable fullness." It was read in the
little mission station at Chin-kiang on Saturday, September 4,
1869. The missionary was always reticent about telling details
of his transforming experience; but he did say, "As I read, I saw
it all. I looked to Jesus; and when I saw, oh how the joy
flowed!"

His fellow missionaries said of him, "Mr. Taylor went out,
a new man in a new world, to tell what the Lord had done for
his soul."

Let the man of God speak for himself regarding *the life that
is Christ*. Writing to his sister in England he said:

"As to work, mine was never so plentiful, so responsible, or
so difficult; but the weight and strain are all gone. The last
month or more has been perhaps, the happiest of my life; and
I long to tell you a little of what the Lord has done for my soul.
I do not know how far I may be able to make myself intelligi-
ble about it, for there is nothing new or strange or wonderful—

and yet, all is new! In a word, 'Whereas once I was blind, now I see . . .'

"When my agony of soul was at its height, a sentence in a letter from dear McCarthy was used to remove the scales from my eyes, and the Spirit of God revealed the truth of our oneness with Jesus as I had never known it before. McCarthy, who had been much exercised by the same sense of failure, but saw the light before I did, wrote (I quote from memory): 'But how to get faith strengthened? Not by striving after faith, but by resting on the Faithful One.'

"As I read I saw it all! 'If we believe not, He abideth faithful.' I looked to Jesus and saw (and when I saw, oh, how joy flowed!) that He had said, 'I will never leave you.' 'Ah, there is rest!' I thought. 'I have striven in vain to rest in Him. I'll strive no more. For has He not promised to abide with me—never to leave me, never to fail me?' And, dearie, He never will!

"But this was not all He showed me, nor one half. As I thought of the Vine and the branches, what light the blessed Spirit poured into my soul! How great seemed my mistake in having wished to get the sap, the fullness out of Him. I saw not only that Jesus would never leave me, but that I was a member of His body, of His flesh and of His bones. The vine now I see, is not the root merely, but all—root, stem, branches, twigs, leaves, flowers, fruit: and Jesus is not only that: He is soil and sunshine, air and showers, and ten thousand times more than we have ever dreamed, wished for, or needed. Oh, the joy of seeing this truth! I do pray that the eyes of your understanding may be enlightened, that you may know and enjoy the riches freely given us in Christ. . . .

"The sweetest part, if one may speak of one part being sweeter than another, is the rest which full identification with Christ brings. I am no longer anxious about anything, as I realize this; for He, I know, is able to carry out His will, and His will is mine. It makes no matter where He places me, or how. That is rather for Him to consider than for me; for in the easiest positions He must give me His grace, and in the most difficult His grace is sufficient."

God's grace is indeed sufficient, and the heart that has come to know personally and intimately the risen Lord Jesus by the outflow of His spirit experiences the reality of "rivers of living water." With Isaiah he knows that "thou wilt keep him in perfect peace whose mind is stayed on thee, because he trusteth in thee."

Many years after Hudson Taylor's meeting with the Lord Jesus in "the little crowded house in Chin-kiang," an Anglican clergyman, the Reverend H. B. Macartney of Melbourne, Australia, added this testimony to that of many others regarding the missionary's possession of the *life that is Christ:*

"He was an object lesson in quietness. He drew from the Bank of Heaven every farthing of his daily income—'My peace I give unto you.' Whatever did not agitate the Savior, or ruffle His spirit was not to agitate him. The serenity of the Lord Jesus concerning any matter and at its most critical moment, this was his ideal and practical possession. He knew nothing of rush or hurry, of quivering nerves or vexation of spirit. He knew there was a peace passing all understanding, and that he could not do without it.

"Now I was altogether different. Mine is a peculiarly nervous disposition, and with a busy life I found myself in a tremor all day long. I did not enjoy the Lord as I knew I ought. Nervous agitation possessed me as long as there was anything to be done. The greatest loss of my life was the loss of the light of the Lord's presence and fellowship during writing hours. The daily mail robbed me of His delightful society.

"'I am in the study, you are in the big spare room,' I said to Mr. Taylor at length. 'You are occupied with millions, I with tens.

Your letters are pressingly important, mine of comparatively little moment. Yet I am worried and distressed, while you are always calm. Do tell me what makes the difference.'

"'My dear Macartney,' he replied, 'the peace you speak of is in my case more than a delightful privilege, it is a necessity.'

"He said most emphatically, 'I could not possibly get through the work I have to do without the peace of God "which passeth all understanding" keeping my heart and mind.'

"'Keswick teaching' as it is called was not new to me at that time. I had received those glorious truths and was preaching them to others. But here was the real thing—an embodiment of 'Keswick teaching' such as I had never hoped to see. This impressed me profoundly:—here is a man almost sixty years of age, bearing tremendous burdens, yet absolutely calm and unruffled. Oh, the pile of letters! any one of which might contain news of death, or shortness of funds, or riots or serious trouble. Yet all were opened, read and answered with the same tranquillity—Christ his reason for peace, his power for calm. Dwelling in Christ he partook of His very being and resources, in the midst of and concerning the very matters in question. And he did this by an act of faith as simple as it was continuous.

"Yet he was delightfully free and natural. I can find no words to describe it save the Scriptural expression 'in God.' He was 'in God' all the time, and God in him. It was that true 'abiding' of John 15."

With good reason could the clergyman add the exhortation to all: "Are you in a hurry, flurried, distressed? Look up! See the Man in the Glory! Let the face of Jesus shine upon you—the face of the Lord Jesus Christ. Is He worried, troubled, distressed? There is no wrinkle on His brow, no least shade of anxiety. Yet the affairs are His as much as yours."

It is the abiding life that is fruitful, just as it is the soul drinking deeply of the water of life that realizes "shall never thirst." The *life that is Christ* is abiding and abounding, it is sat-isfying and overflowing. Hudson Taylor could not find words more adequate to express the truth of the Scriptures he had proved by experience than those in the little booklet by Harriet Beecher Stowe, *How to Live on Christ,* a copy of which he sent to every member of the mission. In part Mrs. Stowe stated:

"How does the branch bear fruit? Not by incessant effort for sunshine and air; not by vain struggles for those vivifying influences which give beauty to the blossom, and verdure to the leaf: it simply abides in the vine, in silent and undisturbed union, and blossoms and fruit appear as of spontaneous growth.

"How, then, shall a Christian bear fruit? By efforts and struggles to obtain that which is freely given; by meditations on watchfulness, on prayer, on action, on temptation, and on dangers? No: there must be a full concentration of the thoughts and affections on Christ; a complete surrender of the whole being to Him; a constant looking to Him for grace. Christians in whom these dispositions are once firmly fixed go on calmly as the infant borne in the arms of its mother. Christ reminds them of every duty in its time and place, reproves them for every error, counsels them in every difficulty, excites them to every needful activity. In spiritual as in temporal matters they take no thought for the morrow; for they know that Christ will be as accessible tomorrow as today, and that time imposes no barrier on His love. Their hope and trust rest solely on what He is willing and able to do for them; on nothing that they sup-pose themselves able and willing to do for Him. Their talisman for every temptation and sorrow is their oft-repeated child-like surrender of their whole being to Him."

Such is the "exchanged life," the abiding, fruitful life, *the life that is Christ,* which should be the possession of every believer. Galatians 2:20 should be, and can be, a glorious reality.

I am crucified with Christ: nevertheless I live; yet not I, but
Christ liveth in me: and the life which I now live in the flesh
I live by the faith of the Son of God, who loved me, and gave
himself for me.

Chapter Two

SAMUEL LOGAN BRENGLE
The Cleansed Life

*I*n the Salvation Army, and in every place where he was known, Commissioner Samuel Logan Brengle was loved. No name is more revered among Salvationists than his, for there has been no soldier more saintly nor officer more spiritually effective than this quiet-spoken prophet of God.

He was, indeed, the gift of God to the Army and to the people of God everywhere as an evangelist, bringing salvation to sinners, and holiness of life to the soldiers who carried the Army motto of "Blood and Fire." By life and by lip he urged the living Savior *for* the seeker and *in* the believer.

The secret of Brengle's spiritual effectiveness was the flow of divine life through him, which flow had been made possible because the channel had been cleansed and was kept clean.

Left fatherless by the ravages of the War between the States, he was reared on an Indiana farm by an earnest and godly mother. One Christmas Eve, his mother knelt beside him at the mourners' bench in the little rural Methodist church, and quietly told her lad that he should trust the Savior; and he did. Some time later, as mother and son were walking across a broad prairie and talking about the Savior, there came to young Samuel's heart the witness of the Spirit that, indeed, he was a child of God.

Happy in the activities of Sunday school and church and studious in the Scriptures, he felt he should prepare for college even though in those days few young men aspired to that achievement. After his mother was called to the Savior's presence, and the farm was sold, college became a reality. Then for two years he was a circuit preacher of the Northwest Indiana Methodist Conference, after which he went to Boston for his seminary training.

There were humbling experiences in his first years of ministry, and as a result there came to his heart a hunger for complete consecration to the Savior and for holiness of life. He saw that he himself was his greatest enemy in effective service for the Lord. As he sought the truth of God in the Scriptures and searched his own heart, he found that consecration meant emptying of all that he was in himself before he could be filled with the Spirit. Of that heart searching he wrote:

"I saw the humility of Jesus, and my pride; the meekness of Jesus, and my temper; the lowliness of Jesus, and my ambition; the purity of Jesus, and my unclean heart; the faithfulness of Jesus, and the deceitfulness of my heart; the unselfishness of Jesus, and my selfishness; the trust and faith of Jesus, and my doubts and unbelief; the holiness of Jesus, and my unholiness. I got my eyes off everybody but Jesus and myself, and I came to loathe myself."

His ambition was to be a great preacher; and he sought the power of the Holy Spirit to that end. He rationalized that a great preacher would do more for the glory of God than one who was mediocre. Finally, in utter desperation, he prayed, "Lord, I wanted to be an eloquent preacher, but if by stammering and stuttering I can bring greater glory to Thee than by eloquence, then let me stammer and stutter!"

With the problem of pride settled, there remained the matter of cleansing from sin. His heart was hungry. Though emptied of self and self-seeking, he was not filled with God. Then it was that 1 John 1:9 became clear to him: "If we confess our sins, he is faithful and just to forgive us our sins, and to cleanse us from all unrighteousness."

Years later he recorded his experience in the little volume, *When the Holy Ghost Is come,* in these words:

"I shall never forget my joy, mingled with awe and wonder, when this dawned upon my consciousness. For several weeks I had been searching the Scriptures, ransacking my heart, humbling my soul, and crying to God almost day and night for a pure heart and the baptism with the Holy Ghost, when one glad, sweet day (it was January 9, 1885) this text suddenly opened to my understanding: 'If we confess our sins, He is faithful and just to forgive our sins, and to cleanse us from all unrighteousness'; and I was enabled to believe without any doubt that the precious Blood cleansed my heart, even mine, from all sin. Shortly after that, while reading these words of Jesus to Martha: 'I am the resurrection and the life; he that believeth on Me, though he were dead, yet shall he live; and he that liveth and believeth on Me shall never die,' instantly my heart was melted like wax before fire; Jesus Christ was revealed to my spiritual consciousness, revealed in me, and my soul was filled with unutterable love. I walked in a heaven of love. Then one day, with amazement, I said to a friend: 'This is the perfect love about which the Apostle John wrote; but it is beyond all I dreamed of; in it is personality; this love thinks, wills, talks with me, corrects me, instructs and teaches me.' And then I knew that God the Holy Ghost was in this love and this love was God, for 'God is love.'

"Oh, the rapture mingled with reverential, holy fear—for it is a rapturous, yet divinely fearful thing—to be indwelt by the Holy Ghost, to be a temple of the Living God! Great heights are always opposite great depths, and from the heights of this blessed experience many have plunged into the dark depths of fanaticism. But we must not draw back from the experience through fear. All danger will be avoided by meekness and low-liness of heart; by humble, faithful service; by esteeming oth-ers better than ourselves, and in honor preferring them before ourselves; by keeping an open, teachable spirit; in a word, by looking steadily unto Jesus, to whom the Holy Spirit continu-ally points us: for He would not have us fix our attention exclusively upon Himself and His work *in* us, but also upon the Crucified One and His work *for* us, that we may walk in the steps of Him whose Blood purchases our pardon, and makes and keeps us clean."

The following morning Brengle met on the street a humble man known about Boston as "the Hallelujah coachman," and told him of his experience of a clean heart.

His friend jumped up and down for joy, said Brengle, exclaiming: "Brother Brengle, preach it!" "He and I walked out across Boston common," Brengle continued. "He talked and I listened. He couldn't speak a dozen words without butchering the Queen's English, but I was hungry enough now to listen to anybody. As he talked I took on courage, and said: 'By the grace of God, I will preach it, if they throw me out of the church afterwards!'"

True to his conviction, he preached that truth the follow-ing Sunday in his student church, and gave his testimony. Thereby, he put himself on record that God had cleansed his heart. Some of his audience went out as they came in that morning; others were visibly moved and went forward to say, "Brother Brengle, if that is holiness, we want it."

His biographer, Clarence W. Hall, relates this story:

"Two mornings after his sanctification the honeypots were spilled into his heart. He had honored God; he had stood the test of bearing faithful witness. And since His man has exercised fullness of faith, God would now vouchsafe to him fullness of feeling. He has mirrored this experience for us in the following:

"'I awoke that morning hungering and thirsting just to live this life of fellowship with God, never again to sin in thought or word or deed against Him, with an unmeasurable desire to be a holy man, acceptable unto God. Getting out of bed about six o'clock with that desire, I opened my Bible and, while reading some of the words of Jesus, He gave me such a blessing as I never had dreamed a man could have this side of heaven. It was an unutterable revelation. It was a heaven of love that came into my heart. My soul melted like wax before fire. I sobbed and sobbed. I loathed myself that I had ever sinned against Him or doubted Him or lived for myself and not for His glory. Every ambition for self was now gone. The pure flame of love burned it like a blazing fire would burn a moth.

"'I walked out over Boston Commons before breakfast, weeping for joy and praising God. Oh, how I loved! In that hour I knew Jesus, and I loved him till it seemed my heart would break with love. I was filled with love for all His creatures. I heard the little sparrows chattering; I loved them. I saw a little worm wriggling across my path; I stepped over it; I didn't want to hurt any living thing. I loved the dogs, I loved the horses, I loved the little urchins on the street, I loved the strangers who hurried past me, I loved the heathen—I loved the whole world!'

"Concerning his sanctification," continued Mr. Hall, "of which the 'glory experience' was only an incident, he has given us this record:

"'I have never doubted this experience since. I have sometimes wondered whether I might not have lost it, but I have never doubted the experience any more than I could doubt that I had seen my mother, or looked at the sun, or had my breakfast. It is a living experience.

"'In time, God withdrew something of the tremendous emotional feelings. He taught me I had to live by my faith and not by my emotions. I walked in a blaze of glory for weeks, but the glory gradually subsided, and He made me see that I must walk and run, instead of mounting up with wings. He showed me that I must learn to trust Him, to have confidence in His unfailing love and devotion, regardless of how I felt.'"

And what resulted from the continuance of that crisis experience of cleansing and the filling of God's Spirit? Brengle's preaching changed perceptibly. Before this he had preached for human appreciation, now alone for the exaltation of the Savior. He preached to disturb and not to please. The reaction of his audiences was conviction of sin rather than commendation of the preacher.

Furthermore, the deliverance from pride and ambition for ecclesiastical promotion led him into untrodden pathways of service. From the preferment and security of Methodism he was called into the ranks of the Salvation Army when that organization was little known and not highly regarded.

When he reported at the Army's international headquarters in London on June 1, 1887, he was met by General Booth's calculating comment: "Brengle, you belong to the dangerous classes. You have been your own boss for so long that I don't think you will want to submit to Salvation Army discipline. We are an Army, and we demand obedience."

To this the candidate could only reply: "I have received the Holy Spirit as my sanctifier and guide. I feel He has led me to offer myself to you. Give me a chance."

The training period was torturous but Brengle stood every test. Every morning his first duty was to black the boots of his fellow cadets; and in that lowly service he found sweet fellowship with the Savior. After assignment to various English corps he was sent back to America for service.

The Appointments were to small places, new works: nothing like what he could have expected had he remained a respectable Methodist minister. When stationed in Danbury, Connecticut, he led his little contingent of faithful ones, consisting of a lame lieutenant, a big Negro, and a little hunch-backed girl, to a street meeting to the tune of "We're the Army that Shall Conquer!" Suddenly he came abreast of a large and imposing Methodist church and for a moment red hot were the thoughts that burned through his soul, *Fool, you might have been a pastor of a great church like that!* But the sting was only for a moment, for the Sanctifier steadied the soldier to obey His orders.

Following an attack in the skid row of Boston, when he was struck down by a paving brick thrown by a drunken tough, he devoted his time to writing articles for the *War Cry* of the Army; and later these materials were collected into a helpful little volume entitled, *Helps to Holiness.* In later years, when appreciation was expressed for blessing received from that book, Brengle would smile in reply: "Well, if there had been no little brick, there would have been no little book!"

Mrs. Brengle kept the brick and painted on it the testimony of Joseph: "As for you, [you] thought evil against me; but God meant it unto good . . . to save much people alive" (Gen. 50:20).

The effective evangelism of God's prophet was eloquently stated in the testimony of a prominent pastor in the Southland who wrote:

"In April, 1900 . . . I received a pressing invitation from the officer-in-charge of the local corps of the Salvation Army to attend a three-day revival campaign to be conducted by Colonel S. L. Brengle. I read the circular detailing the meetings, and was impressed by the Colonel's scholarship. I went to the first meeting. His face charmed me, his heart caught me, but his mention of 'holiness' aroused all my combativeness. I had been an opponent of the doctrine of the Second Work of Grace, and considered it illogical, contrary to psychology; etc.

But I could not help being interested by his non-ranting, simple, straightforward handling of the subject. And not only interested, but shall I say, concerned. I invited him to my study for a conference. He came the next morning. I opened my heart to him as I never before had done to any living being. He made very little comment, simply saying, 'I think sanctification will fix you.' That was hard to take.

"But I was at the afternoon meeting. At the conclusion of his sermon, he asked all who wanted a clean heart to stand. I stood, the only one. Then he asked all who wanted to be converted to stand. A poor old drunken toper and a streetwalker stood. Then he invited us to the penitent form. I led the procession, followed by the bum and the wanton woman, and, when presently I looked around, one was on either side of me. It was a bitter pill for the pastor of a large church, graduate of a celebrated school of theology, with some excellent prospects for the ministry, to be thus humiliated. But I determined to make the most of it, and charitably—I thought humbly—including my mates at the penitent form, I began to pray: 'O Lord, we—,' when the Colonel broke in with, 'Not we, brother, pray for yourself!' I prayed for myself, made the consecration after Brengle had dealt gently but definitely with me—the while being careful, I thought, to avoid a debative approach—and at the next meeting testified modestly to the Blessing. He said, 'I am glad for that testimony, brother. Don't be afraid of terms, don't be afraid of the Second Blessing.'

"Thus it was through his instrumentality that I entered into the Canaan of Perfect Love. His skill and wisdom and approach made possible results that no logic or arguments could have produced, though his addresses were logical itself. I regard him with almost worshipful love. I owe more to him than to any man alive. I have often thought that God sent him to Birmingham purposely to bless me."

Even to his closing days, in his seventy-sixth year, Commissioner Brengle found that the life of God continued to flow through a cleansed heart. Body began to fail and sight grew more faint, yet God's servant could say: "My old eyes get dimmer, the specialist says the light will fade altogether. So I gird myself for darkness, quote James 1:2–4, shout 'Hallelujah' and go on!"

Later, when speaking engagements had to be canceled because of the gathering darkness, he could testify:

". . . I have sweet fellowship at times in my own room. The saints of all the ages congregate there. Moses is present, and gives his testimony, and declares that the eternal God is his refuge and underneath are the everlasting arms.

"Joshua arises, and declares, 'as for me and my house, we will serve the Lord.' Samuel and David, my dear friends Isaiah, Jeremiah, and Daniel, Paul and John and James, and deeply humbled and beloved Peter, each testify to the abounding grace of God. Luther and Wesley and the Founder [General William Booth] and Finney, and Spurgeon and Moody, and unnumbered multitudes all testify.

"Blind old Fanny Crosby cries out: 'Blessed assurance, Jesus is mine!' So, you see, I am not alone. Indeed, I can gather these saints together for a jubilant prayer and praise meeting almost any hour of the day or night. Hallelujah forever, and glory to God!"

It was "hallelujah!" all the way, even to his last murmured words (the quoting of Ps. 34), for the holiness of God flooded his life. Since that meeting with the Savior in seminary days there had continued with him the unfailing Presence, the preciousness of God's salvation, and the power of His Spirit, with perseverance to the end; and all because of purification of heart.

Chapter Three

JOHN BUNYAN
The Unchained Life

*I*t could rightly be said that Bedford's tinker is one of those "of whom the world is not worthy." Like the apostle Paul, who recognized himself as "the prisoner of the Lord" and not of the Roman government, John Bunyan, though bound with chains for preaching the truth of God, was in spirit free. Like Paul also, Bunyan's writings have lived through the centuries, and wherever the Bible has gone in hundreds of translations Bunyan's *Pilgrim's Progress* has followed.

Few men have been so deeply taught in the Scriptures as was Bunyan, and none has surpassed him as a master of allegory. The "House of the Interpreter" remains one of the world's best schoolrooms. Bunyan's characters are familiar everywhere: Christian, who found his burden removed at the cross, and Christiana with her four sturdy sons; also Faithful, Hopeful, Evangelist and Interpreter, Great Heart and Mr. Standfast. Others include Mr. Talkative, Mr. By-ends, and Giant Despair and his wife Diffidence, and Ignorance who reached heaven's gate only to find he had no scroll for admittance.

Literature and speech abound with the places made known in *Pilgrim's Progress:* the Hill Difficulty and the Palace Beautiful at its crest, Forgetful Green and By-path Meadow, Vanity Fair, and Doubting Castle, the River of Death and the City of the Great King.

Bunyan was born of humble parents; and although they put

him into school for a time he learned so little that later he forgot how to read and write, until his wife taught him anew. As a youth he was disturbed by dreams and fears and, though mercifully delivered from death by drowning and again while in military service, he grew up godless, careless and so greatly given to blasphemy that he was a source of terror to others. Underneath his appearance of unconcern about his spiritual welfare, however, there was a hunger for God. One day while pursuing his trade as a tinker he observed "three or four poor women sitting at a door in the sun talking about the things of God," and being now willing to hear about God he drew near to listen. "Their talk was about a *new birth,* the work of God in their hearts. . . . They talked how God had visited their souls with his love in the Lord Jesus. . . ." Bunyan did not understand what they meant, but was "greatly affected with their words."

He made repeated efforts at self reformation. He was admired by others for his ceasing to swear. He thought that the task of ringing the church bell would gain merit for him, but he found no inner change; rather, he became apprehensive that the church bell might fall on him. Now that he was married and had learned to read he began to go through the Scriptures, but found no understanding of them. He received help from a Mr. Gifford, a godly pastor in that area, who undoubtedly is represented in *Pilgrim's Progress* as Evangelist.

Bunyan was puzzled about the doctrine of election and troubled by blasphemous thoughts. He was given to frequent depressions and was under sore temptation by the enemy of mankind to "sell Christ!" Finally, in despair of gaining Christ, he said, "Let Him go if He will!"

Thereafter, the statement in Hebrews 12:17 regarding Esau filled him with dismay, for the Scriptures said: "Ye know how that afterward, when he would have inherited the blessing, he was rejected; for he found no place of repentance, though he sought it carefully with tears."

Bunyan would gain brief encouragement by remembering that Peter repented and was received back by the Savior; then the dreadful words about Esau would dash him to the ground. There was nothing on earth that he desired so much as assurance of forgiveness and salvation. But where could it be found?

John 6:37—"and him that cometh to me, I will in no wise cast out"—was the scriptural key that unlocked the bondage brought on by his blasphemy. It sweetly visited his soul, and he said: "Oh! the comfort that I found from this word, *In no wise!* As if he had said, By no means, for nothing, whatever he hath done. But Satan would greatly labour to pull this promise from me by telling me that Christ did not mean me and such as I, but sinners of a lower rank, that had not done as I had done. But I would answer him again, 'Satan, there is in these words no such exception: but *him that cometh, him, any him; him that cometh to me,* I will in no wise cast out. . . .' If ever Satan and I did strive for any word of God in all my life, it was for this good word of Christ; he at one end, and I at the other. Oh! what work we made! It was for this in John, I say, that we did so tug and strive; he pulled and I pulled; but, God be praised, I overcame him; I got sweetness from it."

Although at long length Bunyan had deep inner assurance of acceptance with God, he was still unsettled in his mind and deeply troubled by that Scripture about Esau. Quietly and painstakingly the Spirit of God taught him that Esau despised the birthright and afterward was refused the blessing. Thus he learned that "the birthright signified regeneration, and the blessing the eternal inheritance. . . ." That those who despise regeneration will be denied heaven he understood correctly.

Other Scripture also disturbed him, such as Hebrews 10:26: "For if we sin willfully after that we have received the knowledge of the truth, there remaineth no more sacrifice for sins." He learned, however, that his sin was not that open denial of the Savior and casting off His commandments, and thereby he was comforted.

The crisis of the deeper life came to Bunyan one day as he was walking in the fields. "Suddenly," he said, "this sentence fell upon my soul, *Thy righteousness is in heaven*. And me thought, with awe, I saw, with the eyes of my soul, Jesus Christ at God's right hand; there, I say, was my righteousness; so that wherever I was, or whatever I was doing, God could not say of me, He wants my righteousness, for that was just before him. I also saw, moreover, that it was not my good frame of heart that made my righteousness better, nor yet my bad frame that made my righteousness worse; for my righteousness was Jesus Christ himself, 'the same yesterday, today, and forever,' Hebrews 13:8."

Forcefully and with finality the Holy Spirit presented to Bunyan the reality of the risen Savior who "is made unto us wisdom, and righteousness, and sanctification, and redemption." Therefore with delight he could say:

"Now did my chains fall off my legs indeed I was loosed from my afflictions and irons; my temptations also fled away; so that from that time those dreadful scriptures of God left off to trouble me. . . .

"Oh! me thought, Christ! Christ! there was nothing but Christ that was before my eyes. I was not now only for looking upon this and the other benefits of Christ apart, as of his blood, burial, or resurrection; but considering him as a whole Christ, as he in whom all these and all other virtues, relations, offices and operations met together, and that he sat on the right hand of God in heaven. It was glorious to me to see his exultation, and the worth and prevalency of all his benefits. . . ."

Thus it was that Bunyan learned the wonderful reality of "the life that is Christ." Ephesians 5:30 became "a sweet word" to him: "For we are members of his body, of his flesh, and of his bones." He could say: "Further, the Lord did also lead me into the mystery of union with the Son of God. . . . By this also was my faith in him, as my righteousness, the more confirmed in me; for if he and I were one, then his righteousness was mine, his merits mine, his victory also mine. Now I could see myself in heaven and earth at once; in heaven by my Christ, by my head, by my righteousness and life, though on earth by my body or person."

In much the same manner the victory came to Charles G. Trumbull nearly three hundred years later, as we shall see when we consider the experience that led him to the life that wins.

And what were the results of Bunyan's being unchained from his doubts and fears? In his *Grace Abounding to the Chief of Sinners,* which ranks with *Augustine's Confessions* as among the best spiritual chronicles of that kind, he tells of many results. Among them he lists *grace* that could keep him in deepest difficulties, *insight* into the Scriptures, *no fear* of death, an *assurance* of his Lord's presence with him, and a *fruitful service* for the Savior both in the pulpit and in the prison.

"I never saw such heights and depths in grace, and love, and mercy," he declared. "I had two or three times, at or about my deliverance from this temptation, such strange apprehensions of the grace of God, that I could hardly bear up under it; and it was so out of measure amazing, when I thought it could reach me, that I do think if that sense of it had abode long upon me it would have made me incapable for business."

Whereas before he had been perplexed with unbelief, blasphemy, and hardness of heart, he could say, "Now was God and Christ continually before my face. . . . The glory of the holiness of God did at this time break me to pieces. . . ."

He added, when facing a deep testing, "As I was sitting by the fire I suddenly felt this word to sound in my heart: *I must go to Jesus.* At this my former darkness and atheism fled away, and the blessed things of heaven were set in my view. . . . That night was a good night to me, I have had but few better; I long for the company of some of God's people, that I might impart unto them what God had showed me. Christ was a precious Christ to my soul that night; I could scarce lie in my bed for joy, and peace, and triumph, through Christ."

The fears that had beset him about death were banished; and he could testify: "I saw myself within the arms of grace and mercy; and though I was before afraid to think of a dying hour, yet, now I cried, Let me die; now death was lovely and beautiful in my sight, for I saw we shall never live indeed until we be gone to the other world. . . . God himself is the portion of his saints. This I saw and wondered at, but cannot tell you what I saw."

His neighbors and friends were aware of a great change in his life, and urged him to preach the Word to them, and to others. He was timid to do so but then was persuaded that God had given him the ministry of preaching and teaching. At first his message was altogether about sin and the Savior. ". . . the terrors of the law and guilt from my transgressions lay heavy on my conscience; I preached what I felt, what I smartingly did feel. . . . Indeed, I have been as one sent to them from the dead; I went myself in chains, to preach to them in chains; and carried that fire in my own conscience that I persuaded them to be aware of."

Then his preaching took on more of an exaltation of "Jesus Christ in all his offices, relations and benefits unto the world;" then he began to teach "the mystery of the union of Christ." After five years of fruitful ministry, in which many found the Savior, he was imprisoned; but during those two terms in Bedford Jail he completed the immortal allegories of *Pilgrim's Progress* and *The Holy War.*

"The Scriptures also were wonderful to me," he stated earnestly after he had learned the reality of union with the risen Savior; "I saw that the truth and verity of them were the keys of the kingdom of Heaven." While in prison he could write: "I never had in all my life so great an inlet into the Word of God as now: those Scriptures that I saw nothing in before are made in this place and state to shine before me; Jesus Christ also was never more real and apparent than now. . . .

"I never knew what it was for God to stand by me at all times, and at every offer of Satan to afflict me, as I have found him since I came in hither; for, lo! as fears have presented themselves, so have supports and encouragements; yea, when I have started even as it were at nothing else but my shadow, yet God, as being very tender of me, hath not suffered me to be molested, but would with one Scripture or another strengthen me against all; insomuch that I have often said, were it lawful I could pray for greater trouble for greater comfort sake."

Bunyan's insight into the Scriptures by the teaching of the Holy Spirit is nowhere better illustrated than in his description of the entrance of Christian and Hopeful into the city of the Great King. By many it is regarded as the finest piece of writing in the English language as well as a magnificent presentation of Scriptural truth. Sit beside Bunyan in Bedford's prison, and read as he writes:

"Now, upon the bank of the river, on the other side, they saw the two shining men again, who there waited for them. Wherefore, being come out of the river, they saluted them, saying, 'We are ministering spirits, sent forth to minister for those that shall be heirs of salvation.' Thus they went along towards the gate.

"Now you must note, that the city stood upon a mighty hill; but the pilgrims went up that hill with ease, because they had these two men to lead them up by the arms; they had likewise left their mortal garments behind them in the river; for though they went in with them, they came out without them. They therefore went up here with much agility and speed, though the foundation upon which the city was framed was higher than the clouds; they therefore went up through the region of the air, sweetly talking as they went, being comforted because they safely got over the river, and had such glorious companions to attend them.

"The talk that they had with the shining ones was about the glory of the place; who told them that the beauty and glory of it was inexpressible. There, said they, is Mount Sion, the heavenly Jerusalem, the innumerable company of angels, and the spirits of just men made perfect. . . . The men then asked, What must we do in the holy place? To whom it was answered, You must there receive the comfort of all your toil, and have joy for all your sorrow; you must reap what you have sown, even the fruit of all your prayers, and tears, and sufferings for the King by the way. In that place you must wear crowns of gold, and enjoy the perpetual sight and vision of the Holy One; for 'there you shall see him as he is.' There also you shall serve him continually with praise, with shouting and thanksgiving, whom you desired to serve in the world, though with much difficulty, because of the infirmity of your flesh. There your eyes shall be delighted with seeing, and your ears with hearing the pleasant voice of the Mighty One. There you shall enjoy your friends again that are gone thither before you; and there you shall with joy receive even every one that follows into the holy place after you. . . .

"Now, while they were thus drawing towards the gate, behold a company of the heavenly host came out to meet them: to whom it was said by the other two shining ones, These are the men that have loved our Lord when they were in the world, and that have left all for his holy name; and he hath sent us to fetch them, and we have brought them thus far on their desired journey, that they may go in and look their Redeemer in the face with joy. . . .

"Now I saw in my dream, that these two men went in at the gate; and lo, as they entered, they were transfigured; and they had raiment put on that shone like gold. There were also that met them with harps and crowns, and gave them to them; the harps to praise withal, and the crowns in token of honour. Then I heard in my dream, that all the bells in the city rang again for joy, and that it was said to them,

ENTER YE INTO THE JOY OF YOUR LORD

I also heard the men themselves, that they sang with a loud voice, saying,

BLESSING, AND HONOUR, AND GLORY, AND POWER, BE UNTO HIM THAT SITTETH UPON THE THRONE, AND UNTO THE LAMB, FOREVER AND EVER.

"Now, just as the gates were opened to let in the men, I looked in after them, and behold the city shone like the sun; the streets also were paved with gold; and in them walked many men, with crowns on their heads, palms in their hands, and golden harps, to sing praises withal.

"There were also of them that had wings, and they answered one another without intermission, saying, Holy, holy, holy is the Lord. And after that they shut up the gates: which, when I had seen, I wished myself among them."

Bedford's blasphemous tinker had become God's best thinker and dreamer who, by union with the risen Savior, found life unchained.

Chapter Four

AMY CARMICHAEL
The Radiant Life

$\mathscr{A}$my Carmichael first met the living Lord on the streets of
Belfast. She was just a girl then, in her teens. The meeting with
the Savior was sudden and startling, wholly unexpected. In
Gold Cord, the autobiographical account of the background
and the building of the Christian home for girls and boys at
Dohnavur in South India, she relates the meeting, as important
in her life as was the revelation of the Lord Jesus to Saul of
Tarsus on the way to Damascus.

"It was a dull Sunday morning," she recalled, "in Belfast. My
brothers and sisters and I were returning with our mother from
church when we met a poor pathetic old woman who was carrying a heavy bundle. We had never seen such a thing in
Presbyterian Belfast on Sunday, and, moved by sudden pity, my
brothers and I turned with her, relieved her of the bundle, took
her by her arms as though they had been handles, and helped
her along. This meant facing all the respectable people who
were, like ourselves, on their way home. It was a horrid
moment. We were only two boys and a girl, and not at all exalt-
ed Christians. We hated doing it. Crimson all over (at least we
felt crimson, soul and body of us) we plodded on, a wet wind
blowing us about, and blowing, too, the rags of that poor old
woman, till she seemed like a bundle of feathers and we unhap-
pily mixed up with them. But just as we passed a fountain,

recently built near the kerbstone, this mighty phrase was suddenly flashed as it were through the grey drizzle:

"'Gold, silver, precious stones, wood, hay, stubble; every man's work shall be made manifest; for the day shall declare it, because it shall be revealed by fire; and the fire shall try every man's work of what sort it is. If any man's work abide. . . .'

"*If any man's work abide*—I turned to see the voice that spoke with me. The fountain, the muddy street, the people with their politely surprised faces, all this I saw, but nothing else. The blinding flash had come and gone, the ordinary was all about us. We went on. I said nothing to anyone, but I knew that something had happened that had changed life's values. Nothing could ever matter again but the things that were eternal."

That afternoon the eighteen-year-old Amy shut herself in her room, talked to God, and settled once and for all the pattern of her future life. Amy had found the Lord Jesus as her personal Savior two years before when a student at school in Harrogate, North Ireland. In the moments of quiet at the conclusion of an evangelistic meeting, the Good Shepherd, she said, "answered the prayers of my father and mother and many other loving ones, and drew me, even me, into His fold."

At the age of nineteen she attended a convention in Glasgow. There she heard the "Keswick testimony" of the life of victory by the Holy Spirit for the first time. She recalled:

"I had been longing for months, perhaps years, to know how one could live a holy life, and a life that would help others. I came to that meeting half hoping, half fearing. Would there be anything for me? I don't remember feeling there was anything (my fault) in either of the two addresses. The fog in the hall seemed to soak into me. My soul was in a fog. Then the chairman rose for the last prayer. Perhaps the previous address had been about Peter walking on the water, and perhaps it had closed with the words of Jude 24, for the one who prayed began like this, *'O Lord, we know Thou art able to keep us from falling.'* Those words found me. It was as if they were alight, and they shone for me."

In exaltation of mind and spirit she left the meeting and went with her hostess to a restaurant for lunch. "The mutton chop wasn't properly cooked and somebody said so," wrote Amy Carmichael. "I remembered wondering, 'Whatever does it matter about mutton chops? *O Lord, we know Thou are able to keep us from falling.'"*

Assurance of salvation at Harrogate ("the one watered moment in an arid three years"), awareness of eternal values by the Holy Spirit at Belfast ("something had happened that had changed life's values"), and the actuality of the new life in Christ at Glasgow ("Thou are able to keep us from falling")— these were the spiritual milestones of Amy Carmichael's awakening and preparation for her long and fruitful service for the Lord Jesus.

Early did this Irish girl learn the sensitivity to the Holy Spirit that is indispensable in a close walk with God. Still in her teens she was led to Christian service in a Belfast mission, "The Welcome." For some nights there were souls saved night after night, then suddenly the meetings went dead. As she prayed and searched her own heart she remembered "a rollicking hour when we reached home after the meeting and, as usual, it was my fault. There was nothing wrong in the fun, *but it was not the time for it.* I have never forgotten the shock of that discovery. *Grieve not the Spirit,* that was the word then. In His mercy He forgave; and the work went on again."

There was the implicit and wholehearted response to the call for foreign service, quite unthought of even the day before it came, on January 13, 1892. Obedient to that call of *Go Ye* she was appointed the first missionary under the Keswick convention and within a few months went to Japan. Though her service there was brief she learned many lessons that were invaluable later in the fifty-five consecutive years that she served in India.

Not long after she arrived in Japan, she learned the importance of simplicity of dress and appearance on the part of missionaries and the value of adaptability to the clothing and the standards of the people among whom one had come to witness for the Savior.

It was a hard lesson, learned in a sad way. With her Christian fellow worker, Misaki San, she had gone to visit an old lady who was ill. In response to Miss Carmichael's word, translated by Misaki San, the needy heart seemed just about to turn to the Savior when the lady noticed fur gloves on the missionary's hands and was distracted from the message. "I went home," said the young missionary, "took off my English clothes, put on my Japanese *kimono,* and never again, I trust, risked so very much for the sake of so very little. . . ."

Another valuable lesson came out of that experience. Said Miss Carmichael: "The touch of that old lady on my fur gloves set free, though I never imagined it, thousands of hours of time; for the saving of time is great when a company of people live for many years without having to spend any time in giving thought to their clothes. And it set free hundreds of pounds; for the saving of money is also great, when at a stroke all the extras of dress are cut off, and nothing need be spent on them. And all this time and money saved has meant just so much the more to give to Him Who gave us all. But more than that, as I believe, it led to the opening of doors never opened before. It would have been impossible for one in foreign dress to go to the places to which I had to go if I were ever to discover the truth about things in India. And more, far more than that, it opened doors to hearts. If any question that, I can fall back on this: it made it just a little less easy for the great enemy to distract a soul who was drawing near to its Savior."

Early in her missionary life she also learned the strength of the Strong One. A Buddhist neighbor in the Japanese village of Matsue was possessed by the "Fox spirit," as they called it. The Japanese knew the reality of demon possession but had heard nothing of deliverance from that dreadful bondage. Miss Carmichael and Misaki San went uninvited to pray for a demon-possessed man, only to be driven away, but not before they had assured the wife that they would pray at home until her husband was delivered from the power of the Fox spirit. Within an hour a messenger came to say that all the Foxes, six of them, were gone; and the next day the man, perfectly well, came with a branch of pomegranate flowers to express his appreciation for their prayers. Some months later he died of malaria, peacefully, with his New Testament clasped in his hands. Thus she learned in actual combat that "greater is he that is in you than he that is in the world."

Such was the beginning of her deep acquaintance with the Lord and her preparation for service in India. One day in India, while sitting under a wide-spreading tree with her Tamil grammar and dictionary before her, she became conscious of the "unfolding sense of a Presence, a Listener." It seemed to her He looked for some to listen with Him, to listen to the voice of one's brother's blood crying to Him from the ground. Time ceased for the lady under the tree and she sat all that day in His presence. That day on the hillside influenced all the years that were to follow for Amy Carmichael, and gave depth to them all.

When she was called by the Lover of little children to the rescuing of girls from the temple, and later of boys in danger, few missionaries or Indian Christians were in sympathy with her. Of this she wrote: "Sometimes it was as if I saw the Lord Jesus Christ kneeling alone, as He knelt long ago under the olive trees. The trees were tamarind now, the tamarinds that I see as I look up from this writing. And the only thing that one who cared could do, was to go softly and keel down beside Him, so that He would not be alone in His sorrow over the little children."

The sensitivity to spiritual and eternal values gave her not only insight to discern the presence of her Lord, but also outer sight to "see things as they are." The publication of a volume by that name, *Things As They Are,* in 1903, caused tremendous stir in India, and also in Britain: so much so that a committee on the field was appointed to ask her to return to England. She found, however, that the Lord of the Harvest overruled in her behalf when others misunderstood her obedience to marching orders and her understanding of the battle.

She had by the Holy Spirit a wonderful gift of teaching others to trust the Faithful One. When the First War brought great hardship and uncertainty to the work in Dohnavur there were opportunities to help the children learn the simplicity and sweetness of faith in God. In her 1915 diary we read:

"October 26. Had children in field weeding. Told them of need of money—a new idea to them. Explained a little to older girls about our way of working, and what it involved of careful sensitiveness towards God. Finally got them, and all, to the point of willingness to give today (Festival Day) to weeding. Girls splendid over it, children very sweet and good. Inwardly prayed for a quick assurance from our Father that He was pleased. It would be like Him to do this.

"October 27. Mail in today, and 50 from a friend of Irene Streeter, the soldier brother's money left to her. Took letter up to field where children were weeding, and we all praised God standing in shadow of cactus hedge. There was other money too—more in one mail than has come for many months. All much cheered, and much awed too."

The Spirit-filled life is a practical one. Amy Carmichael found it so. In the problem of guidance she learned to pray, to trust, to obey, and not to look back.

"When decisions have to be made, don't look back and wonder what I would have done. Look up, and light will come to do what our Lord and Master would have you do.

"It may be that decisions which seem to change the character of the work will have to be made. But if the root principles which have governed us from the beginning are held fast, there will be no real change. The river may flow in a new channel, but it will be the same river.

"If you hold fast to the resolve that in all things Christ as Lord shall have the pre-eminence, if you keep His will, His glory, and His pleasure high above everything, and if you continue in His love, loving one another as He has loved you, then all will be well, eternally well."

Amy Carmichael had a singing heart. Sensitive, artistic, and radiant, her gift of song found expression in her poetry. Few writers in our generation have had the ministry of pen in poetry and also prose as has Amy Carmichael of Dohnavur. These responses of her heart to trials of faith and triumphs of God's faithfulness have been printed and reprinted in every quarter of the globe.

One poem will suffice to illustrate all the rest:

From prayer that asks that I may be
Sheltered from winds that beat on Thee,
From fearing when I should aspire,
From faltering when I should climb higher,
From silken self, O Captain, free
Thy soldier who would follow Thee.

From subtle love of softening things,
From easy choices, weakenings,
Not thus are spirits fortified,
Not this way went the Crucified,
From all that dims Thy Calvary,
O Lamb of God, deliver me.

Give me the love that leads the way,
The faith that nothing can dismay,
The hope no disappointments tire,
The passion that will burn like fire,
Let me not sink to be a clod:
Make me Thy fuel, Flame of God.

And what shall we say of her books: *Things As They Are, Meal in a Barrel, Gold Cord, If,* and *Though the Mountains Shake,* to mention just a few?

In *Gold Cord,* Amy Carmichael tells of a trip one hot September day by some happy Indian children to trace their mountain river to its remote source. To them it seemed no difficulty to follow the ravine upward and onward until the unfailing font was found. The climb was long and exciting, through the forest glades where tiny hoof prints were noted by the water's edge, and even a trace of a tiger.

"The children found new delights," she writes, "fairy falls and fairy pools and caves and dear growing things, great ferns and cushions of moss; but the source they did not find. A tree had crashed through the forest just where the banks were too steep to climb and the undergrowth was too entangled to penetrate. The trunk was covered with orchids, and was a beautiful thing, but it barred the way. Below it was a deep, clear pool. The children knew that, far beyond, above the fringes of the forest, the real source must lie out under the sky in a lonely loveliness, with only the wind and the whispering rushes and the marsh flowers to tell it of the ways of the world below. But they could not go up there."

Such was a parable of Amy Carmichael. The ultimate source of her overflowing life was far beyond, out of sight and reach, because it was in God. The "pool" from which her life poured forth was the meeting with the Lord Jesus on Belfast's rainy streets with its challenging words that changed all of life's values: *if any man's work abide!*

Chapter Five

OSWALD CHAMBERS
The Highest Life

ℐf Oswald Chambers ever chose a life motto, it should have been "Excelsior!"

He was never content with low achievement. He was always climbing. Would he ever arrive at any given destination?

His early life seemed to be marked by sunless valleys and steep grades that demanded arduous endeavor. Early efforts produced no sense of success. Gifted in art, he won a scholarship that provided two years of study at famous art centers on the continent. After considering that some men are wrecked in body and soul from studies of that kind, he refused the scholarship.

With a view to preparing for a business career he entered Edinburgh University, but did not remain there long. His friends were persuasive that he was making a foolish choice in transferring to the little known Dunoon Bible Training College. He seemed to be drifting more than climbing.

But he had begun to climb. To family and friends he wrote: "Do not be sorry that I cannot go in for a university curriculum, maybe I shall be best without it. 'Seekest thou great things for thyself? Seek them not.' But although I cannot give myself a university training, I will to the limit of my power educate myself for His sake. Oh, how much weaning it will take, how much discipline! before my life shines forth with the deep passion of my soul 'for the sake of Jesus Christ.'"

The Bible college life at Dunoon "based on the simplicity of daring faith in God for the provision of needs" became the groundwork of Chambers' life of faith and obedience. He came to know by experience that God answers prayer. Likewise there was created in his innermost being a hunger and thirst that only the living God can satisfy. That deep desire, almost fathomless, he struggled to express in his diary:

"The Holy Spirit must anoint me for the work, fire me, and so vividly convince me that such and such a way is mine to aim at, or I shall not go, I will not, I dare not; I shall just be content to earn my living—but, no, that cannot be. From my very childhood the persuasion has been that of a work, strange and great, an experience deep and peculiar, it has haunted me ever and ever. . . . Here is the lamb and the wood, but where is the fire? Nothing but the fire of the most Holy Spirit of God can make the offering holy and unblameable and acceptable in His sight."

It was at that time, when his "soul was in turmoil," that he wrote these lines:

> Let me climb, let me climb, I'm sure I've time
> 'Ere the mist comes up from the sea,
> Let me climb in time to the height sublime,
> Let me reach where I long to be.

The Almighty creates no desires deep in the human soul that He cannot Himself satisfy. Oswald Chambers aspired to the alpine peaks of spiritual victory and vision, but could he ever attain the utmost height?

Climbing in the Spirit is accomplished by kneeling, and not by running; by surrender, and not by determination. Despair of self leads to utter desperation; but beyond these mists lies the sunshine of God's presence. Many a soul will turn back to accustomed marshlands of defeat rather than brave the fogs of frustration; but the mountain peaks rise high above the rain and gloom.

This pattern in the crisis of the deeper life, followed by its wide outreach, is almost identical with the experience of countless others of God's children. First, there is the hunger of heart, often followed by a sense of desperation that leads to utter surrender of self. Thereafter there is the meeting of the soul with God in whatever manner the Almighty is pleased to reveal Himself to the desperate seeker who, like Jacob at Jabbok, *will not let Him go until there is blessing.*

To Oswald Chambers there came the day of utter yielding and absolute abandonment to God on every point. As a lad he had come to the Savior and had enjoyed the presence of the Lord Jesus. Years passed, however, before he came to the plateau of spiritual fullness from which he could continue climbing in the sunshine to God's highest for his life.

"I was in Dunoon College as a tutor in philosophy," he recalled, "when Dr. F. B. Meyer came and spoke about the Holy Spirit. I determined to have all that was going, and went to my room and asked God simply and definitely for the baptism of the Holy Spirit, whatever that meant. From that day on for four years, nothing but the overruling grace of God and kindness of friends kept me out of an asylum.

"God used me during those years for the conversion of souls, but I had no conscious communion with Him. The Bible was the dullest, most uninteresting book in existence, and the sense of depravity, the vileness and bad-motivedness of my nature, was terrific. I see now that God was taking me by the light of the Holy Spirit and His Word through every ramification of my being.

"The last three months of those years things reached a climax, I was getting very desperate. I knew no one who had what I wanted; in fact I did not know what I did want. But I knew that if what I had was all the Christianity there was, the thing was a fraud. Then Luke 11:13 got hold of me—'If ye then, being evil, know how to give good gifts to your children: how much more shall your heavenly Father give the Holy Spirit to them that ask Him?'

"But how could I, bad motivated as I was, possibly ask for the gift of the Holy Spirit? Then it was borne in upon me that I had to claim the gift from God on the authority of Jesus Christ and testify to having done so. But the thought came— if you claim the gift of the Holy Spirit on the word of Jesus Christ and testify to it, God will make it known to those who know you best how bad you are in heart. And I was not willing to be a fool for Christ's sake. But those of you who know the experience, know very well how God brings one to the point of utter despair, and I got to the place where I did not care whether everyone knew how bad I was; I cared for nothing on earth, saving to get out of my present condition.

"At a little meeting held during a mission in Dunoon, a well known lady was asked to take the after meeting. She did not speak, but set us to prayer, and then sang 'Touch me again, Lord.' I felt nothing, but I knew emphatically my time had come, and I rose to my feet. I had no vision of God, only a sheer dogged determination to take God at His word and to prove this thing for myself, and I stood up and said so.

"That was bad enough, but what followed was ten times worse. After I had sat down the lady worker, who knew me well, said: 'That is very good of our brother, he has spoken like that as an example to the rest of you.'

"Up I got again and said: 'I got up for no one (else's) sake, I got up for my own sake; either Christianity is a downright fraud, or I have not got hold of the right end of the stick.' And then and there I claimed the gift of the Holy Spirit in dogged committal on Luke 11:13.

"I had no vision of heaven or of angels, I had nothing. I was as dry and empty as ever, no power or realization of God, no witness of the Holy Spirit. Then I was asked to speak at a meeting, and forty souls came out to the front. Did I praise God? No, I was terrified and left them to the workers, and went to Mr. MacGregor (a friend) and told him what had happened, and he said: 'Don't you remember claiming the Holy spirit as a gift on the word of Jesus, and that He said: "Ye shall receive power . . . ?" 'This is the power from on high.' Then like a flash something happened inside me, and I saw that I had been wanting power in my own hand, so to speak, that I might say—Look what I have by putting my all on the altar.

"If the four previous years had been hell on earth, these five years have truly been heaven on earth. Glory be to God, the last aching abyss of the human heart is filled to overflowing with the love of God. Love is the beginning, love is the middle and love is the end. After He comes in, all you see is 'Jesus only, Jesus ever.'

"When you know what God has done for you, the power and the tyranny of sin is gone and the radiant, unspeakable emancipation of the indwelling Christ has come, and when you see men and women who should be princes and princesses with God bound up by the show of things—oh, you begin to understand what the Apostle meant when he said he wished himself accursed from Christ that men might be saved!"

It was with implicit obedience that Oswald Chambers learned, on the basis of Luke 11:13, that *by faith* we receive the fullness of God's Spirit, just as by faith we receive the Lord Jesus as Savior.

And what did the immediacy of God mean in the life of Oswald Chambers? He himself said again and again, "It is no wonder that I talk so much about an altered disposition: God altered mine; I was there when He did it. . . ."

As was true of the prophets of old, Chambers was a man of God, but not unapproachable nor other-worldly. He was personable and practical, and yet a dreamer, a thinker with a long-range view. A pastor wrote of him: "In friendly intercourse he was one of the most genial and attractive of men. The children in the home loved him and his boyish ways. . . . Yet he was a mighty unflinching messenger of God. He never obtruded his views upon others, but when men sought further knowledge, they soon found they were in the presence of a master mind."

He was a man of prayer, interceding, imploring, and believing. He had rare insight into the meaning of the Scripture, and from this came pointed and practical preaching. Derogatory speaking on the part of others did not deflect his spirit from following his Savior, who likewise knew what it meant to be "despised and rejected of men." He was literally "a bond slave of Jesus Christ"; and yet none knew more glorious liberty as a child of God.

He was an intriguing teacher of the Word; he loved the Word and loved his students. One of them declared: "To say that he took a keen interest in his students is to understate the case; he positively adapted his lectures to our mental capacities, and helped us in private with what we could not understand in class. His enthusiasm knew no bounds. He could never do things by halves. . . ."

He was passionately devoted to the Lord Jesus Christ. He walked with God and inspired all who knew him to believe that real life was to know God and Jesus Christ whom He had sent. Because he himself walked with the Highest, his students learned also to follow in that pathway. One of them declared: "He introduced us to Jesus Christ, never to himself. . .he never made it easy, never offered us an alternative."

The absorbing passion of his life was utter abandonment to the Lord Jesus and to His will. That abandonment gave him an inner calm and quiet that was constant and consistent. Outwardly he was tireless in teaching, writing, witnessing, praying. He was led to service for the Savior in America and in Japan where his Spirit-filled messages the Almighty used to transform many lives.

He was called to teach at the Dunoon Bible Training College in 1911, which responsibility he filled with signal sweetness and blessing. In July 1915 he was appointed to YMCA overseas service with the British troops in Egypt. In a hut at Zeitoun he ministered to the material and spiritual needs of the Tommies, who were guarding the all-essential Suez Canal.

The kindly and tireless concern for the welfare of his men brought out even deeper lessons from the Scriptures, it seems, than he had taught in the sheltered and quiet environment in England. The duties in Egypt were exhausting, though in spirit he was exuberant and exhilarating.

While General Allenby and the expeditionary force were engaged in the successful campaign to free Jerusalem and Palestine from the age-old domination of the Turk, this faithful servant at Zeitoun was called to higher service. A strange providence of God, it may seem to us, that Oswald Chambers should conclude his ministry on earth, while still in his forties; but the ways of Him who knoweth best are past finding out.

The title of Oswald Chambers' best known volume, *My Utmost For His Highest,* epitomizes his walk with God. That devotional book of daily readings is perhaps as widely read as any volume of its kind; and although it has gone through more than twenty printings it is still in great demand. The secret of its perennial freshness and effectiveness is the touch of eternity detected therein by the fellow pilgrim who is seeking God.

A simple headstone in the military cemetery in old Cairo marks his last earthly resting place. On this tone, engraved for all to read, is the testimony of his life, not in his words or those of family or friends, but rather this statement, majestic in its simplicity, taken from Luke 11:13—"How much more will your heavenly Father give the Holy Spirit to them that ask him?"

Chapter Six

CHARLES GRANDISON FINNEY
The Powerful Life

A farmer lad on fire, an Elijah among lawyers, a pungent and powerful preacher of penitence, such was Charles G. Finney. Born in rural Connecticut after the Revolutionary War, reared in a backwoods area of central New York State, he was successively a school teacher and a lawyer before he became a preacher of the gospel.

Finney's conversion was sudden, startling, dramatic, and dynamic. Through his youth he had received so little Christian instruction that at the age of twenty-nine he found himself as ignorant of the gospel as a heathen. He did not understand Bible terms, and although some believers labored to show him Christian doctrine he was not convinced. Nevertheless he believed the Bible to be the Word of God. That confidence led him to a reading of the Scriptures, which in turn gave him concern about the salvation of his soul.

Of his tremendous sense of need, his despair, and of overwhelming victory, Finney tells his own story far better than anyone else could. "On a Sabbath evening in the autumn of 1821, I made up my mind that I would settle the question of my soul's salvation at once, that if it were possible I would make my peace with God. But as I was very busy in the affairs of the office, I knew that without great firmness of purpose, I should never effectually attend to the subject. I therefore then and there resolved, as far as possible, to avoid all business, and everything that would divert my attention, and to give myself wholly to the work of securing the salvation of my soul. I carried this resolution into execution as sternly and thoroughly as I could. I was, however, obliged to be a good deal in the office. But as the providence of God would have it, I was not much occupied either on Monday or Tuesday, and had opportunity to read my Bible and engage in prayer most of the time. . . ."

"During Monday and Tuesday my convictions increased; but still it seemed as if my heart grew harder. I could not shed a tear; I could not pray. I had not opportunity to pray above my breath; and frequently I felt that if I could be alone where I could use my voice and let myself out, I should find relief in prayer. I was shy, and avoided, as much as I could, speaking to anybody on any subject. I endeavored, however, to do this in a way that would excite no suspicion, in any mind, that I was seeking the salvation of my soul.

"Tuesday night I had become very nervous; and in the night a strange feeling came over me as if I was about to die. I knew that if I did I should sink down to hell; but I quieted myself as best I could until morning.

"At an early hour I started for the office. But just before I arrived at the office, something seemed to confront me with questions like these: indeed, it seemed as if the inquiry was within myself, as if an inward voice said to me, 'What are you waiting for? Did you not promise to give your heart to God? And what are you trying to do? Are you endeavoring to work out a righteousness of your own?'

"Just at this point the whole question of gospel salvation opened to my mind in a manner most marvelous to me at the time. I think I then saw, as clearly as I ever have in my life, the reality and fullness of the atonement of Christ. I saw that His work was a finished work; and then instead of having, or needing, any righteousness of my own to recommend me to God, I had to submit myself to the righteousness of God through Christ. Gospel salvation seemed to me to be an offer of something to be accepted; and that it was full and complete; and that all that was necessary on my part, was to get my own consent to give up my sins, and accept Christ. Salvation, it seemed to me, instead of being a thing to be wrought out, by my own works, was a thing to be found entirely in the Lord Jesus Christ, who presented Himself before me as my God and my Savior.

"Without being distinctly aware of it, I had stopped in the street right where the inward voice seemed to arrest me. How long I remained in that position I cannot say. But after this distinct revelation had stood for some little time before my mind, the question seemed to be put, 'Will you accept it now, today?' I replied, 'Yes; I will accept it today, or I will die in the attempt.'

"North of the village, and over a hill, lay a piece of woods, in which I was in the almost daily habit of walking, more or less, when it was pleasant weather. It was now October, and the time was past for my frequent walks there. Nevertheless, instead of going to the office, I turned and bent my course towards the woods, feeling that I must be alone, and away from all human eyes and ears, so that I could pour out my prayer to God. . . .

"But when I attempted to pray I found that my heart would not pray. I had supposed that if I could only be where I could speak aloud, without being overheard, I could pray freely. But lo! when I came to try, I was dumb, that is, I had nothing to say to God; or at least I could say but a few words, and those without heart. In attempting to pray I would hear a rustling in the leaves, as I thought, and would stop and look up to see if somebody were not coming. This I did several times.

"Finally I found myself verging fast to despair. I said to myself, 'I cannot pray. My heart is dead to God, and will not pray.' I then reproached myself for having promised to give my heart to God before I left the woods. When I came to pray, I found I could not give my heart to God. My inward soul hung back, and there was no going out of my heart to God. I began to feel deeply that it was too late, that it must be that I was given up of God and was past hope.

"The thought was pressing me of the rashness of my promise, that I would give my heart to God that day or die in the attempt. It seemed to me as if that was binding upon my soul; and yet I was going to break my vow. A great sinking and discouragement came over me, and I felt almost too weak to stand upon my knees.

"Just at this moment I again thought I heard someone approach me, and I opened my eyes to see whether it were so. But right there the revelation of my pride of heart, as the great difficulty that stood in the way, was distinctly shown to me. An overwhelming sense of my wickedness in being ashamed to have a human being see me on my knees before God, took such powerful possession of me, that I cried at the tope of my voice, and exclaimed that I would not leave that place if all the men on earth and all the devils in hell surrounded me. 'What!' I said, 'such a degraded sinner as I am, on my knees confessing my sins to the great and holy God, and ashamed to have any human being, and a sinner like myself, find me on my knees endeavoring to make my peace with my offended God!' The sin appeared awful, infinite. It broke me down before the Lord.

"Just at that point this passage of Scripture seemed to drop into my mind with a flood of light: *Then shall ye go and pray unto Me, and I will hearken unto you. Then shall ye seek Me and find Me, when ye shall search for Me with all your heart.* I instantly seized hold of this with my heart. I had intellectually believed the Bible before; but never had the truth been in my mind that faith was a voluntary trust instead of an intellectual state. I was as conscious as I was of my existence, of trusting at that moment in God's veracity. Somehow, I knew that that was a passage of Scripture, though I do not think I had ever read it. I knew that it was God's word, and God's voice, as it were, that spoke to me. I cried to Him, 'Lord, I take Thee at Thy word. Now Thou knowest that I do search for Thee with all my heart, and that I have come here to pray to Thee; and Thou hast promised to hear me.'

"That seemed to settle the question that I could then, that day, perform my vow. The Spirit seemed to lay stress upon that idea in the test, *When you search for Me with all your heart.* The question of when, that is, of the present time, seemed to fall heavily into my heart. I told the Lord that I should take Him at His word; that He could not lie; and that therefore I was sure that He heard my prayer, and that He would be found of me. . . .

"I walked quietly toward the village; and so perfectly quiet was my mind that it seemed as if all nature listened. It was on the 10th of October, and a very pleasant day. I had gone into the woods immediately after an early breakfast; and when I returned to the village I found it was dinner time. Yet I had been wholly unconscious of the time that had passed; it appeared to me that I had been gone from the village but a short time. . . .

"I went to my dinner, and found I had no appetite to eat. I then went to the office, and found that Squire W_____ had gone to dinner. I took down my bass viol, and, as I was accustomed to do, began to play and sing some pieces of sacred music. But as soon as I began to sing those sacred words, I began to weep. It seemed as if my heart was all liquid; and my feelings were in such a state that I could not hear my own voice in singing without causing my sensibility to overflow. I wondered at this, and tried to suppress my tears, but could not. I put up my instrument and stopped singing.

"After dinner we were engaged in removing our books and furniture to another office. We were busy in this, and had but little conversation all the afternoon. My mind, however, remained in that profoundly tranquil state. There was a great sweetness and tenderness in my thoughts and feelings. Everything appeared to be going right, and nothing seemed to ruffle or disturb me in the least.

"Just before evening the thought took possession of my mind, that as soon as I was left alone in the new office, I would try to pray again—that I was not going to abandon the subject of religion and give it up, at any rate; and therefore, although I no longer had any concern about my soul, still I would continue to pray.

"By evening we got the books and furniture adjusted; and I made up, in an open fireplace, a good fire, hoping to spend the evening alone. Just at dark Squire W_____, seeing that everything was adjusted, bade me good-night and went to his home. I had accompanied him to the door; and as I closed the door and turned around, my heart seemed to be liquid within me. All my feelings seemed to rise and flow out; and the utterance of my heart was, 'I want to pour my whole soul out to God.' The rising of my soul was so great that I rushed into the room back of the front office, to pray.

"There was no fire, and no light, in the room; nevertheless it appeared to me as if it were perfectly light. As I went in and shut the door after me, it seemed as if I met the Lord Jesus Christ face to face. It did not occur to me then, nor did it for some time afterward, that it was wholly a mental state. On the contrary, it seemed to me that I saw Him as I would see any other man. He said nothing, but looked at me in such a manner as to break me right down at his feet. I have always since regarded this as a most remarkable state of mind; for it seemed to me a reality, that He stood before me, and I fell down at His feet and poured out my soul to Him. I wept aloud like a child, and made such confessions as I could with a choked utterance. It seemed to me that I bathed His feet with my tears; and yet I had no distinct impression that I touched Him, that I recollect.

"I must have continued in this state for a good while; but my mind was too much absorbed with the interview to recollect anything that I said. But I know, as soon as my mind became calm enough to break off from the interview, I returned to the front office, and found that the fire that I had made of large wood was nearly burned out. But as I turned and was about to take a seat by the fire, I received a mighty baptism of the Holy ghost. Without any expectation of it, without ever having the thought in my mind that there was any such thing for me, without any recollection that I had ever heard the thing mentioned by any person in the world, the Holy Spirit descended upon me in a manner that seemed to go through me, body and soul. I could feel the impression, like a wave of electricity, going through and through me. Indeed, it seemed to come in waves and waves of liquid love; for I could not express it in any other way. It seemed like the very breath of God. I can recollect distinctly that it seemed to fan me, like immense wings.

"No words can express the wonderful love that was shed abroad in my heart. I wept aloud with joy and love; and I do not know but I should say, I literally bellowed out the unutterable gushings of my heart. These waves came over me, and over me, and over me, one after the other, until I recollect I cried out, 'I shall die if these waves continue to pass over me.' I said, 'Lord, I cannot bear any more;" yet I had no fear of death.

"How long I continued in this state, with this baptism continuing to roll over me and go through me, I do not know. But I know it was late in the evening when a member of my choir—for I was the leader of the choir—came into the office to see me. He was a member of the church. He found me in this state of loud weeping, and said to me, 'Mr. Finney, what ails you?' I could make him no answer for some time. He then said, 'Are you in pain?' I gathered myself up as best I could, and replied, 'No, but so happy that I cannot live. . . .'

"I soon fell asleep, but almost as soon awoke again on account of the great flow of the love of God that was in my heart. I was so filled with love that I could not sleep. Soon I fell asleep again, and awoke in the same manner. When I awoke, this temptation would return upon me, and the love that seemed to be in my heart would abate; but as soon as I was asleep, it was so warm within me that I would immediately awake. Thus I continued till, late at night, I obtained some sound repose.

"When I awoke in the morning the sun had risen, and was pouring a clear light into my room. Words cannot express the impression that this sunlight made upon me. Instantly the baptism that I had received the night before returned upon me in the same manner. I arose upon my knees in the bed and wept aloud with joy, and remained for some time too much overwhelmed with the baptism of the Spirit to do anything but pour out my soul to God. It seemed as if this morning's baptism was accompanied with a gentle reproof, and the Spirit seemed to say to me, 'Will you doubt? Will you doubt?' I cried, 'No! I will not doubt; I cannot doubt.' He then cleared the subject up so much to my mind that it was in fact impossible for me to doubt that the Spirit of God had taken possession of my soul.

"In this state I was taught the doctrine of justification by faith, as a present experience. That doctrine had never taken any such possession of my mind that I had ever viewed it distinctly as a fundamental doctrine of the gospel. Indeed, I did not know at all what it meant in the proper sense. But I could now see and understand what was meant by the passage,

'Being justified by faith we have peace with God through our Lord Jesus Christ.' I could see that the moment I believed, while up in the woods, all sense of condemnation had entirely dropped out of my mind; and that from that moment I could not feel a sense of guilt or condemnation by any effort that I could make. My sense of guilt was gone; my sins were gone; and I do not think I felt any more sense of guilt than if I never had sinned."

By the Spirit of God Finney came under deep conviction, learned God's plan of salvation, and was born again of the Spirit; then without his knowledge of any such experience was filled to overflowing with that Spirit!

Armed by the reality of regeneration and anointed with an accolade of fire Finney went forth to witness for his new-found Savior. By the Spirit he had power to witness effectively wherever he went. On the day after his conversion he spoke with many of his neighbors and friends, and could say, "I believe the Spirit of God made lasting impression upon everyone of them. I cannot remember one whom I spoke with who was not soon after converted." His law office companion, Judge Wright, was the first to come to the Savior. Upon Finney's asking grace at the table in a home, an ungodly young man there present retired to his room, and in the morning came out a believer in Christ. Finney observed, "The word of God had a wonderful power; and I was every day surprised to find that a few works spoken to an individual would stick in his heart like an arrow."

By the Spirit Charles Finney became a man of prayer, and then quite spontaneously a preacher of the gospel. He began witnessing and preaching in little school houses and country churches. In his *Memoirs* he recalled, "The Holy Spirit was upon me, and I felt confident that when the time came for action I should know what to preach. . . . The spirit of God came upon me with such power, that it was like opening a battery upon them. For more than an hour, and perhaps for an hour and a half, the Word of God came through me to them in a manner that I could see was carrying all before it.... The Holy spirit fell upon the congregation in a most remarkable manner. A large number of persons dropped their heads, and some groaned so that they could be heard throughout the house." Cataclysmic changes followed the powerful revival labors of Finney from the frontier areas of America to the British Isles. A convert in Rochester, New York, left a description of Finney's revival ministry in that city in which more than a hundred thousand came to saving knowledge of the Lord Jesus within one year. He wrote: "The whole community was stirred. Religion was the topic of conversation, in the house, in the shop, in the office, and on the street.... The only theater in the city was converted into a livery stable; the only circus into a soap and candle factory. Grog shops were closed; the Sabbath was honored; the sanctuaries were thronged with happy worshipers; a new impulse was given to every philanthropic enterprise; the fountains of benevolence were opened, and men lived to do good."

The report continues: "It is worthy of special notice that a large umber of leading men of the place were among the converts—the lawyers, the judges, physicians, merchants, bankers, and master mechanics. These classes were more moved from the very first than any other. Tall oaks were bowed as by the blast of the hurricane. Skeptics and scoffers were brought in, and a large number of the most promising young men. It is said that no less than forty of them entered the ministry....

"It is not to much to say that the whole character of the city was changed by that revival," wrote this eyewitness. "Most of the leaders of society being converted, and exerting a controlling influence in social life, in business, and in civil affairs, religion was enthroned as it has been in few places.... Even the courts and the prisons bore witness to its blessed effects. There was a wonderful falling off in crime. The courts had little to do, and the jail was nearly empty for years afterward."

Finney's powerful preaching against sin and his stirring presentation of the claims of Christ may have seemed harsh to some but in reality this man of God was of a tender spirit. He was a man of tears and great tenderness. In the latter part of his ministry he experienced deep heart-searching by the Spirit, as described in his *Memoirs:* "The Lord gave my own soul a very thorough overhauling, and a fresh baptism of His Spirit.... I gave myself to a great deal of prayer. After my evening services, I would retire as early as I well could; but rose at four o'clock in the morning, because I could sleep no longer, and immediately went to the study, and engaged in prayer.... My days were spent, so far as I could get time, in searching the Scriptures; I read nothing all that winter but my Bible; and a great deal of it seemed new to me.... the whole Scripture seemed to be all ablaze with light, and not only light, but it seemed as if God's Word was instinct with the very life of God.... At this time it seemed as if my soul was wedded to Christ, in a sense in which I had never had any thought or conception of before. The language of the Song of Solomon was as natural to me as my breath. I thought I could understand well the state of mind he was in, when he wrote that song; and concluded then, as I have ever thought since, that that song was written by him after he had been reclaimed from his great backsliding. I not only had all the freshness of my first love, but a vast accession to it. Indeed, the Lord lifted me so much above anything that I had ever experienced before, and taught me so much of the meaning of the Bible, of Christ's relations, and power, and willingness, that I often found myself saying to him, 'I had not known or conceived that any such thing was true.'"

Finney's experience of God was dramatically different from that of most servants of the Savior; and yet it cannot be denied or overlooked. The Spirit of God, like the wind, does blow where He desires; and He does fill the heart of an evangelist with the fire of God.

Chapter Seven

ADONIRAM JUDSON GORDON
The Disciplined Life

*B*oston's Adoniram Judson Gordon was a man mighty in word and in deed. Massive in appearance, masterful in intellect, he was ceaselessly active in the Savior's service, always willing to help a good cause or a downtrodden sinner. He was of a radiant sweet spirit, saintly, patient, exemplary, a lover of mankind, and especially of little children. Delivered from contentiousness, he contended, as a true saint, for the faith "once delivered." Criticism he endured with a courage and calmness that seemed like complacency.

Scholar and preacher, author and Bible teacher who left us a rich heritage of faith and good works in the books he wrote and the Bible college he founded, he was always reticent in telling of God's deep dealing with his own soul and particularly in regard to the crisis of the deeper life. One summer at a Northfield conference, Dr. Gordon with Dwight L. Moody spoke to a group of college students at a consecration service. In a letter to Mrs. Gordon he wrote: "The questions which they asked about the work of the Holy Spirit are the hardest I have to answer. Questions of experience are so much more difficult than questions of doctrine. For while 'the testimony of the Lord is sure' the testimony of consciousness is variable, like the impression on the sea beach, which the next wave may change. So after Mr. Moody had given his experience of the baptism of the Spirit because the students called for it, I confessed to much shrinking and reluctance when they made the same demand of me. The boys would have all that could be known, both of doctrine and experience. A hungrier crowd one rarely finds; may the Lord give us more and more to tell. . . ."

In his spiritual autobiography, *How Christ Came to Church*, Dr. Gordon made reference to the growing drudgery and desperation of spirit that was his experience in the ministry. The record of this deep exercise of spirit is familiar to many of us. He wrote:

"Well do we remember those days when drudgery was pushed to the point of desperation. The hearers must be moved to repentance and confession of Christ; therefore more effort must be devoted to the sermon, more ours to elaborating its periods, more pungency put into its sentences, more study bestowed on its delivery. And then came the disappointment that few, if any, were converted by all this which had cost a week of solid toil. And now attention was turned to the prayer meeting as the possible seat of the difficulty—so few attending it and so little readiness to participate in its services. A pulpit scourging must be laid on next Sunday, and the sharpest sting which words can effect put into the lash. Alas, there is no increase in the attendance, and instead of spontaneity in prayer and witnessing there is a silence which seems almost like sullenness! Then the administration goes wrong and opposition is encountered among officials, so that caucusing must be undertaken to get the members to vote as they should. Thus the burdens of anxiety increase while we are trying to lighten them, and should-be helpers become hinderers, till discouragement comes and sleepless nights ensue; these hot boxes on the train of our activities necessitating a stop and a visit of the doctor, with the verdict overwork and the remedy absolute rest.

"It was after much of all this," he continued, "of which even the most intimate friends knew nothing, that there came one day a still voice of admonition, saying, *There standeth one among you whom ye know not.* And perhaps I answered, 'Who is he, Lord, that I might know him?' I had known the Holy Ghost as a heavenly influence to be invoked, but somehow I had not grasped the truth that he is a Person of the Godhead who came down to earth at a definite time and who has been in the church ever since, just as really as Jesus was here during the thirty and three years of his earthly life. . . ."

With lightening heart came the climax: ". . . how many true Christians toil on, bearing burdens and assuming responsibilities far too great for their natural strength, utterly forgetful that the mighty Burden-bearer of the world is with them to do for them and through them that which they have undertaken to accomplish alone! Happy also for these if some weary day the blessed Paraclete, the invisible Christ, shall say to them, *Have I been so long time with you and yet hast thou not known me?* So it happened to the writer. The strong Son of God revealed himself as being evermore in his church, and I knew him, not through a sudden burst of revelation, not through some thrilling experience of instantaneous sanctification, but by a quiet, sure, and steady discovery, increasing unto more and more. Jesus in the Spirit stood with me in a kind of spiritual epiphany and just as definitely and irrevocably as I once took Christ crucified as my sinbearer I now took the Holy Spirit for my burden-bearer."

A close personal friend, the late George C. Needham, gave the only first-hand account, of which I know, about the "enduement for service" for God's servant.

"Dr. Gordon, unlike some Christians, believed there was something always beyond. This he ever sought to attain. Fifteen years ago, during the first Northfield convention, he was desirous to secure what he yet needed as a saint and servant of Christ. Toward the close of those memorable ten days, spent more in prayer than in preaching, my beloved friend joined me

in a midnight hour of great heart-searching and infilling of the
Spirit. He read with peculiar tenderness our Lord's intercessory
prayer of John 17. The union of the believer with Christ and the
Father, as taught by out Lord in that chapter, called out fervent
exclamations, while with deep pathos he continued reading.
During united prayer which followed the holy man poured out
his soul with a freedom and unction indescribable. I never
heard him boast of any spiritual attainment reached during the
midnight hour. Soul experiences were to him very sacred, and
not to be rehearsed on every ordinary occasion. But I have no
doubt that he received then a divine touch which further enno-
bled his personal life and made his ministry of ever-increasing
spirituality and of ever-widening breadth of sympathy."

After thus meeting the risen Savior and receiving by faith
the filling of the Spirit, Dr. Gordon hurried to a preaching
appointment in Seabright, New Jersey. One who knew him
there has left for us this further word:

"I remember his once coming from Northfield after the
August conference. He seemed filled with the Spirit; he could
not talk commonplaces. He said he had had a great blessing.
He went to his room, and came out shortly after and said he
was going down to the fisher village, and asked the way. He did
not come back until we were at dinner—that hot afternoon.
He had visited the beer and liquor saloons and prayed with the
men there, and had been among the shanties. I know more
than one family saved that day."

The infilling of God's Spirit was not an ecstasy to be kept
selfishly; rather, it was the dynamic of discipleship that constrained a Great Heart to seek humble fisher folk and hopeless
drunkards that they might know the living Savior as their own.
Few preachers and teachers of the Word have been more clear
and convincing on the crisis of the deeper life than was
Dr.Gordon. Let him speak for himself.

"'Then you received the baptism of the Holy Spirit, did you?' some one will ask. Well, we prefer not to use an expression which is not strictly biblical. The great promise, 'Ye shall be baptized in the Holy Ghost' was fulfilled on the day of Pentecost once for all, as it seems to us. Then the Paraclete was given for the entire dispensation, and the whole church present and future was brought into the economy of the Spirit, as it is written: 'For in one Spirit were we all baptized into one body' (1 Corinthians 12:13, R.V.). But for God to give is one thing; for us to receive is quite another. 'God so loved that he gave his only begotten son,' is the word of our Lord to Nicodemus. But it is written also: 'As many as *received* him to them gave he power to become the sons of God.' In order to realize regeneration and sonship it is absolutely essential for us to receive as for God to have given. So on the day of Pentecost the Holy Spirit, as the comforter, Advocate, Helper, and Teacher and Guide, was given to the church. The disciples who before had been regenerated by the Spirit, as is commonly held, now received the Holy Ghost to qualify and empower them for service. It was another and higher experience than that which they had hitherto known. It is the difference between the Holy Spirit for renewal and the Holy Spirit for ministry. Even Jesus, begotten by the Holy Ghost and therefore called 'the son of God,' did not enter upon his public service till he had been 'anointed,' or 'sealed,' with that same Spirit through whom he had been begotten. So of his immediate apostles; so of Paul, who had been converted on the way to Damascus. So of the others mentioned in the Acts, as the Samaritan Christians and the Ephesian disciples (19:1–8). And not a few thoughtful students of Scripture maintain that the same order still holds good; that there is such a thing as receiving the Holy Ghost in order to qualify for service. It is not denied that many may have this blessing in immediate connection with their conversion, from which it need not necessarily be separated. Only let it be marked that as the giving of the Spirit by the Father is plainly spoken of, so distinctly is the receiving of the Spirit on the part of the disciples constantly named in Scripture. . . .

"God forbid," said Gordon, "that we should lay claim to any higher attainment than the humblest. We are simply trying to answer, as best we may from Scripture, the question asked above about the baptism of the Holy Ghost. On the whole, and after prolonged study of the Scripture, we cannot resist this conviction: As Christ, the second person of the Godhead, came to earth to make atonement for sin and to give eternal life, and as sinners must receive him by faith in order to have forgiveness and sonship, so the Holy Spirit, the third person of the Godhead, came to the earth to communicate the 'power from on high;' and we must as believers in like manner receive him by faith in order to be qualified for service. Both gifts have been bestowed, but it is not what we have but what we know that we have by a conscious appropriating faith, which determines our spiritual wealth. Why then should we be satisfied with 'the forgiveness of sins, according to the riches of his grace' (Ephesians 1:7), when the Lord would grant us also 'according to the riches of his glory, to be strengthened with might by his Spirit in the inner man'? (Ephesians 3:16)."

With his usual felicity of expression, Dr. Gordon gave a very apt illustration:

"Just in front of the study window where I write is a street, above which it is said that a powerful electric current is constantly moving. I cannot see that current: it does not report itself to hearing, or sight, or taste, or smell, and so far as the testimony of the senses is to be taken, I might reasonably discredit its existence. But I see a slender arm, called the trolley, reaching up and touching it; and immediately the car with its heavy load of passengers moves along the track as though seized in the grasp of some mighty giant. The power had been there before, only now the car lays hold of it or is rather laid hold of by it, since it was a touch, not a rip, through which the motion was communicated. And would it be presumptuous for one to say that he had known something of a similar contact with not merely a divine force but a divine person? The change which ensued may be described thus: Instead of praying constantly for the descent of a divine influence there was now a surrender, however imperfect, to a divine and ever-present Being; instead of a constant effort to make use of the Holy Spirit for doing my work there arose a clear and abiding conviction that the true secret of service lay in so yielding to the Holy Spirit that he might use me to do his work. . . ."

The dynamic for discipleship is indeed the gift of God, even the Holy Spirit; yet it is costly to our human nature, even death to self.

"It costs much," said Dr. Gordon in one of these convention addresses, "to obtain this power. It costs self-surrender and humiliation and the yielding up of our most precious things to God. It costs the perseverance of long waiting and the faith of strong trust. But when we are really in that power, we shall find this difference: that, whereas before it was hard for us to do the easiest things, now it is easy for us to do the hardest."

Dr. Gordon added: "As we become deeply instructed in this matter, we shall learn to pray less about the details of duty and more about the fullness of power. The manufacturer is chiefly anxious to secure an ample head of water for his mills; and, this being found, he knows that his ten thousand spindles will keep in motion without particular attention to each one. It is, in like manner, the sources of our power for which we should be most solicitous, and not the results."

This is the dynamic for discipleship!

Chapter Eight

RICHARD C. HALVERSON
The Burning Life

*T*he letterhead reads simply: "CONCERN, Inc."

There is a byline by way of explanation, and it states: "Putting Confidence in Giving. Not a reservoir—but a channel!"

Letterhead and stationery often reveal something of the personality or character of the one to whom it belongs, and this is decidedly true in this case for concern for others is one of Richard C. Halverson's most conspicuous characteristics. The constraining compassion of Christ that fills his heart to overflowing I have observed from the earliest days of our acquaintance when he came as a transfer student to Wheaton College. The impression has deepened and broadened over the years.

Dick Halverson is a big man: big of heart and hand, of body and spirit, with a large love for God and for the souls of men. He is a man of vision, but not visionary; he is a worker of intense activity, but deep within are reservoirs of quietness. Sanguine, sunny, radiant and realistic, he is a leader of men because he himself is a humble follower of the Good Shepherd.

For twenty years Dick was not concerned with God. Reared in a nominal Christian home in North Dakota, spiritual things had little meaning to him. His ambition was success in the field of drama and entertainment. To achieve that goal he went to Hollywood at the age of 19. Of those days he has said, "I did not go deeply into sin in the grosser sense, yet from the standpoint of pride and self-determination I was certainly rebellious and insubordinate toward God, to say the least."

His story continues in his own words: "Six months of careless living, economic difficulty, and professional disappointment in Los Angeles helped me to see that the direction I was taking could easily lead to self-destruction. Accordingly I 'dropped in' to the church nearest my residence, was readily and warmly received and soon blessed with a group of new friends whose lives were centered in the church and quite the antithesis of what I had known for many years.

"Three months after I entered the Vermont Avenue Presbyterian Church, the Reverend L. David Cowie candidated for its pulpit. Listening to him two Sundays awakened in me a deep desire to possess the indefinable quality which was so obviously in him. I questioned him about this with the result that he led me to faith in Christ.

"Following my conversion," Dick adds, "there were three very definite crises which have decidedly marked my life and ministry. The first occurred five months after I received Christ as my Savior. There was no doubt of the new birth following my talk with Cowie. Within two weeks my life had unconsciously undergone a radical adjustment of which I became aware in retrospect. My motivation, affections and affinities switched 180 degrees. I was literally a new person. Very shortly the implications of faith in Christ began to grip my heart and the conviction crystallized and deepened that God had a very definite plan for my life. Though I was not willing to admit it even to myself, I felt this involved the mission field, evangelism, or the pastorate."

Awareness that God had a plan for his life became increasingly urgent upon young Halverson. The crisis came at the first Bible conference he ever attended. With Pastor Cowie and young people from the church, he went to Mt. Hermon

Conference near San Jose. His burden and bewilderment increased steadily during the first three days of the conference until finally he requested his pastor's permission to return home. The wise preacher consented on the provision that the new convert would try just one more day at the conference. To this Halverson agreed, and was inwardly preparing to leave on the morrow. However, God's hour for him had struck. That evening the late Dr. George S. McCune, pioneer missionary in Korea, was the speaker.

"There were about 800 young people present," recalled Halverson, "but it seemed to me that Dr. McCune spoke directly to me throughout the message. The decision seemed to involve me alone."

Here is Dick's account of what happened: "The issue was very clear; Christ wanted my life in full surrender. I literally broke out in a cold sweat as I realized this. At that moment surrendering to Christ seemed to mean the end of everything I'd ever dreamed of for myself. To me it meant turning my back on everything I had wanted to be and do.

"I left the meeting that night in a terrible condition, having refused to yield to Christ. However I was rushed from there into a cabin prayer meeting during which time God met me in an unusual way. I surrendered to Him as completely as I knew how; and of course experienced the deepest peace and happiness I had ever known.

"This experience of utter yieldedness to the Savior and the consequent joy that filled my life was far more cataclysmic than my conversion. When I returned to Los Angeles my church friends were aware of great changes in my life.

"As a result of that experience, the Holy Spirit has always been real to me. I do not remember having had any specific teaching on the subject at that time, and I certainly was not seeking any sort of an experience of the Spirit; nevertheless, from that night to this present day, the Person, work and reign of the Holy Spirit has been very precious and relevant."

Pastor Cowie, during his student days at Wheaton College, had been deeply taught in the truths of the Holy Spirit by the late Dr. Orien Edward Tiffany who had been chairman of the Division of Social Sciences. Wanting his friend to have the benefit of such training, he urged Halverson to apply to Wheaton for admission. After completing junior college in Los Angeles, Dick enrolled in Wheaton in the fall of 1937. It was my delight to help clarify his curriculum so that he could fulfill all graduation requirements and graduate within two years. To that end he majored in business administration, and all the time took Greek for his foreign language so as to be prepared for Princeton Seminary.

When seminary days were completed, Dick was called to the assistant pastorate at Linwood Presbyterian Church in Kansas City, where the pastor then was Dr. Cowie. Later Halverson was called to the pastorate of First Presbyterian Church, Coalinga, California, where he served for three years. It was in this first regular pastorate that his second deep experience of the Holy Spirit transpired. Let him tell his own story.

"After two years in Coalinga, I entered into a period of disillusionment that became so acute I felt I must leave the ministry unless something happened to alter the situation. This was resolved when after two weeks of intense aloneness and spiritual wrestling accompanied by the feeling that God had put me aside for any further useful service, I finally told the Lord I was going to continue to serve Him the rest of my life whether there were any fruit or blessing in that service, and whether or not He would finally accept me in heaven. Furthermore I was willing to be 'buried' for the rest of my life in Coalinga and serve in obscurity there or anywhere. This was a tremendous hurdle for me for I had become very ambitious. When this was settled, I took a completely new lease on life.

"One month later a group of our Sunday school teachers went to Forest Home Bible Conference in the San Bernardino region of Southern California for a training conference; and I accompanied them. Following the evening meeting on the second day of that conference, I joined them for refreshments and a time of prayer. This being over, I left the groups to return to my cabin.

"However, the way led past Miss Henrietta Mears's cabin; and here I was strangely constrained to enter and pray. As I approached the door, though the cabin was darkened, I realized some were inside praying. Not wishing to disturb them, I waited outside for perhaps ten or fifteen minutes when the absurdity of my position overtook me. It seemed logical that I should join whoever was praying inside. So I opened the door, crossed the room through the darkness to a chair I could see was empty and knelt beside it.

"A long period of silence ensued and I began to feel that they were waiting for me to pray. I began to pray, others followed, and God came down into that cabin. There was no unusual ecstatic or cataclysmic experience, but God visited us in a way none of us had known before. There was weeping and laughter, much talking and planning. What is most clear from that experience is the fact that upon the hearts of us who were in that prayer meeting was laid a burden for the world and a world-wide vision that persists to this day. Through the years that vision has been fulfilled in many respects in detail as we saw it that evening; and the vision remains as fresh and vivid as ever to us.

"In the middle of the night I finally got to my cabin but could not sleep. Under real compulsion I spent time at the typewriter and wrote what later became known as the four commitments of *The Fellowship of the Burning Heart*. These are:

Having come to a personal belief in the Lord Jesus Christ and realizing that the urgency of the hour in which we live demands the highest type of Christian Discipleship, I wish to unite with a band of young people offering themselves as expendables, with a vision of evangelizing the youth of the world for Jesus Christ in the shortest possible time.

I AM COMMITTED TO THE PRINCIPLE that Christian discipleship is sustained solely by God alone through His Spirit; that the abiding life of John 15 is His way of sustaining me. Therefore I pledge myself to a disciplined devotional life in which I promise through prayer, Bible study, and devotional reading, to give God not less than one hour per day. (Psalm 1.)

I AM COMMITTED TO THE PRINCIPLE that Christian Discipleship begins with Christian character. Therefore I pledge myself to holy living, that by a life of self denial and self-discipline, I may emulate those Christ-like qualities of chastity and virtue which will magnify the Lord. (Philippians 1:20, 21.)

I AM COMMITTED TO THE PRINCIPLE that Christian Discipleship exercises itself principally in the winning of the lost to Jesus Christ. Therefore I pledge myself to seek every possible opportunity to witness in order that I may always be engaged in winning someone to Jesus Christ. (Matthew 28:19, Acts 1:8.)

I AM COMMITTED TO THE PRINCIPLE that Christian Discipleship demands nothing less than absolute consecration to Jesus Christ. Therefore I present my body a living sacrifice, utterly abandoned to God. By this commitment, I desire that God's perfect will shall find complete expression in my life; and I offer myself in all sobriety to be expendable for Jesus Christ. (Romans 12:1, 2; Philippians 3:7–14.)

God being my guide I desire to make these commitments to HIM.

Something else became clear to Dick that night. He felt he must resign the pulpit at Coalinga to follow God's further leading. He did not know what the next step would be. The following morning he shared with the group the commitments he had written and his determination to resign from Coalinga. "Imagine my thrill," he said, "when I learned they had been praying all through the night that I would be led to do this!"

All of those present received the commitments and together they pledged themselves to the disciplines involved. A group of them formed a team and went several places that night telling the story of The Fellowship of the Burning Heart that had been formed and its purposes. Everywhere the story was told it was accompanied by unusual blessing from the Spirit.

From this deep experience of God in his life, Halverson returned to Coalinga and tendered his resignation from the church. It was June, 1947, and the resignation was to be effective the following October. In the meantime he had been invited by Dr. Louis D. Evans, Pastor of First Presbyterian Church, Hollywood, to be youth minister in that church, the largest of Presbyterian churches in the United States. After considerable prayer on the matter and declining the invitation several times, he agreed to go to Hollywood for a year's trial. The Holy Spirit confirmed that choice by having him remain there for many years.

It was during the Hollywood Presbyterian days that *CONCERN, Inc.* was born, and the pointed, pungent little paper, *Perspective,* was launched to reach businessmen with gospel truth.

The third deep experience of God in his life occurred at the end of his first year at the Hollywood church. One Sunday when a group was having prayer in a home following the evening service, the conviction came upon all present that a

team of them should go to China the following fall after Bill and
Betty Blackstone, missionaries on furlough from China, had
returned and had sufficient time to prepare for an evangelistic
mission among students. "We covenanted to pray about this,"
says Dick. "The Blackstones returned to China and we continued to pray and to correspond. The result was that I went to
China in November of 1948. It was a disappointment that others were not able to go. God blessed the mission with many
finding Christ at a most strategic time in the affairs of that
nation. Especially was the mission effective among the students.

"One morning we had risen about 4 o'clock for prayer.
While one of the missionaries was praying, the thought
occurred that God wanted me to lay down my life in China
and not return to the States. I disregarded the impression at
first, but it persisted and became so strong . . . and terrifying
. . . that I remained behind in the bedroom after the others had
gone downstairs for breakfast. I remained there until noon at
which time the matter was settled. I promised the Lord I would
gladly lay down my life in China. I fully expected that sacrifice
would be required of me.

"This experience, together with the sum total of the experiences in China that fall and winter, once more radically
changed my ministry. Upon my return to the church and the
young people in Hollywood, God made it plain to me that I
was in the center of His will; but life's values had all been
changed. I was utterly willing to be anything, do anything, say
anything, go any place that He desired, for my life had been
utterly and irrevocably yielded to Him. In a very real sense I
experienced what Paul meant in Philippians 1:21: 'To me to
live is Christ, and to die is gain.'"

Seven and one-half happy and fruitful years of this entirely new kind of ministry were granted to him at the church in
Hollywood. In May of 1956 he was called to the directorship

of International Christian Leadership, with headquarters in Washington, D. C., a strategic place of service. For Richard Halverson life is different, altogether new, wonderful and meaningful, because the old life of self has been exchanged for the new life in Christ.

Chapter Nine

FRANCES RIDLEY HAVERGAL
The Overflowing Life

*A*dvent Sunday, December 2, 1873, marked the crisis of the exchanged life for Frances Ridley Havergal.

Miss Havergal is best known to us by the continuing ministry of her devotional books, such as, *Kept for the Master's Use,* and by her poems which have been set to music: "Who Is on the Lord's Side?"; "Lord, Speak to Me"; "True-Hearted, Whole-Hearted"; and "I Am Trusting Thee, Lord Jesus." This radiant servant of the Lord Jesus was not only a gifted poetess but was also a writer of music, and has left us a heritage of hymn tunes such as *Hermas* and *Onesimus.*

"Fannie," as she was called affectionately by her family and friends, was the youngest of six children of a Church of England clergyman. Both father and mother were earnest and devoted servants of the Lord Jesus, and brought up their children in the nurture and admonition of the Lord. Even as a child, Fannie was observed to be gifted in music and in the writing of excellent little rhymes.

Reared in a godly home, Miss Havergal was never under the illusion that the Christian heritage she enjoyed would suffice but knew rather that she needed a personal experience with the Savior. Even as a child she was aware of the sinfulness of her own heart, she says. But she also says in her autobiography: "I almost enjoyed my naughtiness in a savage kind of way, because I utterly despaired of getting any better, except by being made a Christian."

At the age of thirteen she was "made a Christian." Deeply moved by the conversion experience of a fellow student at boarding school and carefully instructed by one of the teachers there, she committed her soul to the Savior. ". . . and earth and heaven seemed bright from that moment," she said.

As Miss Havergal came to maturity and the beginning of her life's work in literature and music, there came a growing sense of her own inadequacy and of her need of the spiritual life that is "more abundant." In her autobiography she noted: "I had hoped that a kind of table-land had been reached in my journey, where I might walk in the light, without the weary succession of rock and hollow, crag and morass, stumbling and striving; but I seem borne back into all the old difficulties of the way, with many sin-made aggravations. I think the great root of all my trouble and alienation is that I do not now make an unreserved surrender of myself to God; and until this is done I shall know no peace. I am sure of it."

Later, she lamented: "I wish I rejoiced more, not only on my own account, but if I may so say, on *His*, for surely I should praise Him more by both lip and life. Mine has been such a shady Christian life, yet 'He led them forth by the right way' must somehow be true here, though I don't see how. I ought to make one exception; I have learned a real sympathy with others walking in darkness, and sometimes it has seemed to help me to help them."

Still later she wrote: "I love Him distinctly, positively; and I think I loved Him more and longer than I thought, only I dared not own it to myself. Oh, that I loved Him more and more! How I abhor myself for having loved, for loving, so little."

It is often the Lord's way, in dealing with His dear children, to send a challenge to the needy, longing heart through some piece of writing, as John McCarthy's letter was used of the Lord to open Hudson Taylor's eyes to see the way of faith into the "exchanged life." Just so, a small book with the title *All for Jesus* was instrumental in leading Miss Havergal to the crisis of the deeper life.

All for Jesus came to her in the autumn of 1873. She carefully read it, and its contents fixed her attention on the Lord Jesus. The little book set forth the fullness of Christian experience and blessing, the very thing she longed for so earnestly. She was indeed grateful for having loved the Lord Jesus for many years and of having been delighted in His service; but her experience had not been up to the measure of full consecration nor had there been a uniform brightness and continuous enjoyment of His life.

After she had read and reread that little volume she wrote to its author: "I do so long for deeper and fuller teaching in my own heart. *All for Jesus* has touched me very much. . . . I know I love Jesus, and there are times when I feel such intensity of love to him that I have not words to describe it. . . . So I want Jesus to speak to me, to say 'many things' to me, that I may speak for Him to others with real power. It is not knowing doctrine, but *being with* Him, which will give this."

The Almighty does satisfy the longing soul and He does fill it with goodness; and quickly Miss Havergal found this to be true. In reply to a question by her sister, Maria, she testified quietly:

"Yes, it was on Advent Sunday, December 2nd, 1873, I first saw clearly the blessedness of true consecration. I saw it as a flash of electric light, and what you *see* you can never *unsee*. There must be full surrender before there can be full blessedness. God admits you by the one into the other. He Himself showed me all this most clearly. You know how singularly I have been withheld from attending all conventions and conferences;

man's teaching has, consequently, had but little to do with it. First, I was shown that 'the blood of Jesus Christ His Son cleanseth us from all sin,' and then it was made plain to me that He who had thus cleansed me had power to keep me clean; so I just utterly yielded myself to Him, and utterly trusted Him to keep me."

And what was the outflow of that appropriation of the life of the Lord Jesus made by her complete surrender to Him?

There was the constant experiencing of the fruit of the Spirit. There was undiminished and unchanging love for her Savior and for others. There was the joy that "lifted her whole life into sunshine, of which all she had previously experienced was but as pale as passing April gleams, compared with the fullness of summer glory."

There was the peace of God that passes understanding, flowing onward, ever deepening and widening under the teaching of God the Holy Spirit. Within a few weeks came a real test of the reality of that joy when she learned that her publisher in America had gone bankrupt in the panic of 1873. To a friend she could write: "I have just had such a blessing in the shape of what would have been only two months ago a really bitter blow to me; and now it is actual accession of joy, because I find that it does not even *touch* me! . . . Two months ago this would have been a real trial for me, for I had built a good deal on my American prospects, now 'Thy will be done' is not a sigh but only a *song!* I think if it had been all my English footing, present and prospective, as well as the American, that I thus found suddenly gone, it would have been worth it, for the joy it has been to find my Lord so faithful and true to all His promises."

Hers was now the faith that was unfailing and unfaltering. By her radiant life Frances Havergal witnessed to others, and also by her word: "I never find that He fails to respond to trust," she said. "It is indeed 'whatsoever' in its fullness. And now I see that 'able' means *able,* and 'all' means *all.*.... I keep wondering every day what new lovingkindness is coming next! It is such a glorious life! And the really leaving EVERYTHING to Him is so inexpressibly sweet, and surely He does arrange so much better than we could for ourselves, when we leave it all to Him."

Even in physical weakness and in pain she could say gladly: "How infinitely blessed it is to be *entirely* Christ's. To think that you and I are never to have another care or another fear, but that Jesus has undertaken simply everything for us! And isn't it *grand* to have the privilege of being His instruments? It does seem such loving condescension that He should use us."

With others she could share the confidence that "pain is no mystery when looked at in the light of God's holiness, and in the light of *Calvary.*... Pain, as to God's own children, is, truly and really, only blessing in disguise. It is but His chiseling, one of His graving tools, producing the likeness to Jesus for which we long. I never yet came across a suffering (real) Christian who could not *thank* Him for pain!"

Miss Havergal held a sound scriptural basis for the victorious life into which she had entered. To a friend she wrote: "I have long wanted to explain to you and others in writing (which is easier to me to be *clear* in, than in conversation, with its natural interruptions) what I see as to the subject which to me was undoubtedly the portal into a happy life. As to 'perfectionism' or 'sinlessness,' I have all along, and over and over again, said I never did, and do not, hold either. 'Sinlessness' belongs *only* to Christ *now,* and to our glorified state in heaven. I believe it to be not merely an impossibility on earth, but an actual contradiction of our very being, which cannot be 'sinless' till the resurrection change has passed upon us. But being kept from falling, kept from sins, is quite another thing, and the Bible seems to teem with commands and promises about it."

The letter continues: "First, however, I would distinctly state, that it is *only* as, and while, kept by the power of God Himself that we are not sinning against Him; one instant of standing alone is certain fall! But (premising that) have we not been limiting the cleansing power of the precious blood when applied by the Holy Spirit, and also the keeping power of our God? Have we not been limiting 1 John 1:7, by practically making it refer only to 'the remission of sins that are past,' instead of taking the grand simplicity of 'cleanseth us from all sin?'

"'All' is *all;* and as we may trust Him to cleanse from the stain of past sins, so we may trust Him to cleanse from all present defilement; yes, *all!* If not, we take away from this most precious promise, and, by refusing to take it in its fullness, lose the fullness of its application and power. Then we limit God's power to 'keep'; we look at our frailty more than at His omnipotence. Where is the line to be drawn, beyond which He is *not* 'able?' The very *keeping* implies total helplessness without it, and the very cleansing most distinctly implies defilement without it. It was that one word 'cleanseth' which opened the door of a very glory of hope and joy to me.

"I had never seen the force of the tense before," Miss Havergal joyfully explained, "a continual present, always a present tense, not a present which the next moment becomes a past. It *goes on* cleansing, and I have no words to tell how my heart rejoices in it. Not a coming to be cleansed in the fountain only, but a *remaining* in the fountain, so that it may and can go on cleansing."

Because of such reality of the living Lord Jesus in her life, Frances Ridley Havergal continued to be a radiant, overflowing Christian. The glow of her testimony continues to reach Christian hearts everywhere. The glory and peace of the exchanged life is beautifully stated in her triumphant hymn:

Like a River Glorious

Like a river, glorious is God's perfect peace,
Over all victorious in its bright increase;
Perfect, yet it floweth fuller every day,
Perfect, yet it groweth deeper all the way.

Hidden in the hollow of His blessed hand,
Never foe can follow, never traitor stand;
Not a surge of worry, not a shade of care,
Not a blast of hurry touch the spirit there.

Every joy or trial falleth from above,
Traced upon our dial by the Sun of Love.
We may trust Him fully all for us to do;
They who trust Him wholly find Him wholly true.

Chapter Ten

JOHN HYDE
The Prevailing Life

$\mathcal{A}$ngrily John Hyde crumpled the letter and threw it down on the deck of the steamer. He felt sure he was justified in feeling resentful at the content of that letter. Was he not a missionary, already on board ship and leaving the shores of America for India? Was not his father an outstanding clergyman? Was not he a child of the manse, a graduate of a Christian college and of a seminary? Who should tell him that he needed the fullness of the Holy Spirit for effective service abroad? Did this friend think that he had not received the baptism of the Spirit, or that he would think of going to India without this equipment? John Hyde was angry.

But by and by better judgment prevailed and he picked up the letter and read it again. Possibly he did need something that he had not yet received.

It is recorded that as a result of that letter and the question it raised in his mind, John Hyde gave himself to much prayer for the rest of the voyage, praying that he might indeed be filled with the Spirit and know by actual experience what Jesus meant when He said: "Ye shall receive power, when the Holy Ghost is come upon you; and ye shall be my witnesses both in Jerusalem, and in all Judea and Samaria, and unto the uttermost part of the earth."

How the Lord answered that heart cry during the long voyage to India, Hyde gave us no indication, as though the outworking of the Holy Spirit through his life in India would be ample testimony of it.

The first twelve years in India were largely "hidden years," devoted to long periods of intensive language and Bible study. Often troubled by tropical diseases, he nevertheless devoted himself to visitation work in the many villages of his area. He was a faithful undershepherd, seeking the lost for the Good Shepherd. In that service increasingly he was learning to pray effectively for the unsaved and unconcerned.

But the relative barrenness during those years drove him and others of like spirit, to deeper depths of travail in prayer and to wider frontiers of faith. In 1904 a group of missionaries, inspired by Hyde's prayer life, formed the Punjab Prayer Union. Those becoming members were required to sign these five simple yet searching principles:

1. Are you praying for quickening in your own life, in the life of your fellow workers, and in the church?
2. Are you longing for greater power of the Holy Spirit in your own life and work, and are you convinced that you can not go on without this power?
3. Will you pray that you may not be ashamed of Jesus?
4. Do you believe that prayer is the great means for securing this spiritual awakening?
5. Will you set apart one half-hour each day as soon after noon as possible to pray for this awakening, and are you willing to pray *till the awakening comes?*

It is difficult to measure the impact and importance of Hyde's service that came as a result of his Spirit-filled prayer life. All was marked by the greatest simplicity and sincerity. He was utterly and implicitly obedient to the Spirit. On one occasion at a conference when he was scheduled to speak he did not appear until after several hymns had been sung. Then he sat silently in Indian fashion for some time before arising to declare:

"Brothers, I did not sleep any last night, and I have not eaten anything today. I have been having a controversy with God. I feel that he has warned me to come here and testify to you concerning some things that He has done for me, and I have been arguing with Him that I should not do this. Only this evening a little while ago I got peace concerning the matter and have agreed to obey Him, and now I have come to tell you just some things that He has done for me."

As he unburdened his heart in confession of what God had done for him and in him, he said, "Let us have a season of prayer." One who was present at the service stated later, "I remember how the little company prostrated themselves on the mats on their faces in the Oriental manner, and then how for a long time, how long I do not know, man after man rose to his feet to pray, how there was such a confession of sin as most of us had never heard before, and such crying for mercy and help."

To another audience expecting a challenging message on the Holy Spirit Hyde could only say: "I thank God, He has given me no message for you today." Thereupon the chairman added, "The Holy Spirit is the Leader of this meeting."

"The people began to speak as they were moved by the Holy Spirit, and there was liberty but not license. Conviction of sin came over the people like a tidal wave. Many were in great mental agony and intense physical strain as they felt the near presence of God settle on the congregation. Men and women forgot each other as the divine searchlight was flashed on their lives. Some began to confess sins that blazed in their hearts, and others, as they arose to speak, trembled as hidden sins were brought to light."

Then it was that "the sunshine came and flooded the place, and joy was depicted on many countenances. . . ." The fruit of the Spirit is joy.

The fullness of the Holy Ghost in John Hyde's life made him a prayer warrior, a watchman on the walls, as depicted in Isaiah 62:6, 7: "I have set watchmen upon thy walls, O Jerusalem, which shall never hold their peace day nor night; ye that make mention of the LORD, keep not silence. And give him no rest, till he establish, and till he make Jerusalem a praise in the earth."

He was likewise a tireless witness for the Savior. In time he received assurance in prayer that at least one soul would come to the Savior each day during 1908. There were more than 400 converts added that year. The following year the Lord laid two souls a day on his heart, and prayer was fully answered; the following year his faith was enlarged to claim four a day.

On one trip to a distant and tiny village, Hyde came under the persuasion that ten souls would be won to the Lord. En route, he had the native evangelist, with their ox cart, stopped at a cottage of strangers to ask for water. The missionary presented the Savior, and as he pleaded with the family the native worker became insistent that they should go onward. Hyde persisted, however, in his earnest presentation of the Lord, and by the end of the afternoon all nine members of the family had received Christ.

"But what about that one?" was Hyde's reply to the insistence of his native worker that they be on their way. Then it was that the father in the home, just a new Christian himself, brought in a nephew who had been playing outside the house; and all ten were in the fold.

On his way home in 1911, the missionary, in great weakness and painfulness, stopped in the British Isles to visit fellow workers who had been in India. There he learned that the

Amerian evangelist, Dr. J. Wilbur Chapman, and the song leader, Charles M. Alexander, were holding services in a place that seemed spiritually hard, even impossible. Hyde went to Shrewsbury to take up the burden of prayer. Of this Dr. Chapman wrote as follows:

"At one of our missions in England the audience was extremely small, results seemed impossible but I received a note saying that an American missionary was coming to the town and was going to pray God's blessing upon our work. He was known as 'Praying Hyde.'

"Almost instantly the tide turned. The hall was packed, and my first invitation meant fifty men for Jesus Christ. As we were leaving I said, 'My Hyde, I want you to pray for me.' He came to my room, turned the key in the door, dropped on his knees, waited five minutes without a single syllable coming from his lips. I could hear my own heart thumping and beating. I felt the hot tears running down my face. I knew I was with God. Then with upturned face, down which the tears were streaming, he said: 'Oh, God!'

"Then for five minutes at least, he was still again, and then when he knew he was walking with God his arm went around my shoulder and there came up from the depth of his heart such petitions for men as I had never heard before. I rose from my knees to know what real prayer was. . . ."

Such is a portion of the story of John Hyde who became "Praying Hyde," the man who was anointed by the Holy Spirit to pray.

Chapter Eleven

DWIGHT LYMAN MOODY
The Dynamic Life

*H*as there ever been a more enthusiastic, energetic and enterprising soulwinner than Dwight L. Moody?

As soon as the young shoe clerk in Boston came to assurance of faith in the Savior he began to seek others who likewise should be saved. With little education, but with great earnestness, he sought the wanderer and the wicked that they might know the forgiveness of God and newness of life in Christ. He was a layman at work, a witness for the Savior in his place of employment and in all of his associations.

By day and by night Moody was a personal worker, and a promoter of mission Sunday schools, especially for the needy and neglected. In the dreadful days of the War between the States he was active in witnessing among the troops and the prisoners of war, and he served with the Christian Commission in its ministry of mercy to the wounded and dying.

Providentially he was led to the ministry of an evangelist, to present the claims of Christ to large audiences both in America and in the British Isles. He was a dynamo of feverish activity and apparent effectiveness in those early years, yet deep in his own heart there was a dissatisfaction that increased to the point of desperation. As is so often the case, the Almighty used a humble man to bring Moody to the end of his own resources, and then to realize the riches of God's glorious power. This elderly man, whose name history has not recorded, was the first to indicate to the rising evangelist that the anointing of God's Spirit was absent from his ministry. It happened on an occasion when Moody went down from Boston to New York to speak, and while there was invited to address a little Sunday school. In speaking of the incident, Moody said that it probably influenced him more than any other single experience in his life. As he was getting into the carriage to hurry from the Sunday school to another service he was touched on the shoulder by an old man whose white hair was blowing in the wind. With his finger pointing at Moody, he said, "Young man, when you speak again, honor the Holy Ghost." "I got into the carriage," said Moody, "and drove away, but the voice was continually ringing in my ears; yet I did not understand it. It was six months afterwards before God revealed to me the meaning of that message—that I was entirely dependent upon the Holy Spirit. From that day to this, I seldom stand before a great audience where I don't see that old man, with his outstretched finger, and hear his voice, 'Honor the Holy Ghost.'"

In Chicago, there were two godly women, Mrs. Sara A. Cooke and her friend, Mrs. Hawxhurst, who attended Moody's meetings in Farwell Hall, and on whose hearts there came a great burden that this precious man of God be filled with the Spirit. On more occasions than one, Mr. Moody made reference to them, as he did at a meeting in Glasgow:

"I can myself go back almost twelve years and remember two holy women who used to come to my meetings. It was delightful to see them there, for when I began to preach I could tell by the expression of their faces they were praying for me. At the close of the Sabbath evening services they would say to me, 'We have been praying for you.' I said, 'Why don't you pray for the people?' They answered, '*You* need power.' 'I need power,' I said to myself, 'why, I thought I had power.' I had a large Sabbath school, and the largest congregation in Chicago.

There were *some* conversions at that time, and I was in a sense satisfied. But right along these two godly women kept praying for me, and their earnest talk about 'the anointing for special service' set me thinking. I asked them to come and talk with me, and we got down on our knees. They poured out their hearts, that I might receive the anointing of the Holy Ghost. And there came a great hunger in my soul. I knew not what it was. I began to cry as never before. The hunger increased. I really felt that I did not want to live any longer if I could not have this power for service. I kept on crying all the time that God would fill me with His Spirit."

Then came the great Chicago fire. On the evening of that memorable night in 1871 when one-third of the city was laid in ashes and thousands were left homeless, Moody had preached in Farwell Hall. With the institutions which he had founded in ruins, Moody went East to appeal for funds, but he said:

"My heart was not in the work of begging. I could not appeal. I was crying all the time that God would fill me with His Spirit. Well, one day, in the city of New York—oh, what a day!—I cannot describe it, I seldom refer to it; it is almost too sacred an experience to name. Paul had an experience of which he didn't speak for fourteen years. I can only say that God revealed Himself to me, and I had such an experience of His love that I had to ask Him to stay His hand. I went to preaching again. The sermons were not different; I did not present any new truths, and yet hundreds were converted. I would not now be placed back where I was before that blessed experience if you should give me all the world—it would be as the small dust of the balance."

The sermons were not different; but the servant was!

The truths were not new; but now they were pungent and penetrating!

A few had been converted before; now converts came by the hundreds!

Before, it had been the earnest energy and tireless drive of the man; now it was the dynamic of the Holy Spirit!

Moody rapidly became famous in his work for the Lord. Two years after his deep spiritual experience in New York City (he was walking on Wall Street at the time that the Holy Ghost came upon him in special power) he and Ira Sankey went to England. After three years of ministry in the United Kingdom, Moody returned to Chicago.

"The announcement was made," wrote Mrs. Cooke, "that on a certain morning Mr. Moody would speak in Farwell and all the religious elite of the city were there to greet him. The platform was filled with preachers and leaders in the Christian world, but none had a deeper interest than the writer who looked on that scene with trembling solicitude, fearing lest this wonderful popularity and success might have puffed him up in any way. Mr. Moody spoke with more unction than of yore but at the same time in childlike simplicity. When the meeting closed, we noted amid all the congratulations such a look of humility, as though he would gladly have slipped away from it all. His childlike spirit was his shield and defense. Truly, he was 'clothed with humility as with a garment.'"

More and more Moody's preaching became characterized by the spirit of love. Declared the evangelist:

"The only way any church can get a blessing is to lay aside all difference, all criticism, all coldness and party feeling, and come to the Lord as one man; and when the church lives in the power of the thirteenth chapter of First Corinthians I am sure that many will be added daily to the flock of God. I would like to have the church read that chapter together on their knees . . . and, as you do so, pray God to apply it with power. Of late my earnest prayer to God has been that He would help me to save more, and I cannot tell you how wonderfully He has answered my prayer. It seems as if you were all much nearer and dearer to me than ever. My heart goes out to you, and I long to see you all coming constantly to God for a fresh supply of love."

Moody was scriptural and sane in his teaching on the filling of God's Spirit. In his messages delivered at the New York Hippodrome, he preached:

"Now I want this thing clearly understood. We believe firmly that [if] any man ... has been cleansed by the blood, redeemed by the blood, and been sealed by the Holy Ghost, the Holy Ghost dwells in him. And a thought I want to call your attention to is this, that God has got a good many children who have just barely got life, but not power for service. You might say safely, I think, without exaggeration, that nineteen out of every twenty of professed Christians are of no earthly account so far as building up Christ's kingdom; but on the contrary they are standing right in the way, and the reason is because they have just got life and have settled down, and have not sought for power. The Holy Ghost coming upon them with power is distinct and separate from conversion. If the Scripture doesn't teach it I am ready to correct it.

"Let us look and see what God says, and if you will look in the third chapter of Luke you will see that all these thirty years that Christ had been in Nazareth He had been a son, but now the Holy Ghost comes upon Him for service, and He goes back to Nazareth and finds a place where it is written: 'The Spirit of the Lord God is upon me because He hath anointed me to peach the gospel to the poor. He has sent me to heal the broken-hearted, to proclaim liberty to the captive, to recover sight to the blind, and set at liberty them that are bruised.' And for three years we find Him preaching the kingdom of God, casting out devils, and raising the dead, while for thirty years that He was at Nazareth, we hear nothing of Him. He was a son all the while, but now He is anointed for service; and if the Son of

God has got to be anointed, do not His disciples need it, and shall we not seek it, and shall we barely rest with conversion?

"In the 7th chapter of John, 38th and 39th verses, Jesus says, 'He that believeth on Me, as the scripture hath said, out of his belly shall flow rivers of living water. (But this spake He of the Spirit, which they that believe on Him should receive: for the Holy Ghost was not yet given; because that Jesus was not yet glorified.)' Now, do you tell me that Peter and John and James and the rest of those men had not been converted at that time? Had they been three years with the Son of God and had not been born of the Spirit? Had not Nicodemus been born of the Spirit, and had not men been converted before them? Yes, but they were saints without power, and must tarry in Jerusalem until imbued with power from on high. I believe we should accomplish more in one week than we should in years if we had only this fresh baptism. . . .

"It seems to me we have got about three classes of Christians: the first class, in the 3rd chapter of John, were those who had got to Calvary and there got life. They believed on the Son and were saved, and there they rested satisfied. They did not seek anything higher. Then in the 4th chapter of John we come to a better class of Christians. There it was a well of living water bubbling up. There are a few of these, but they are not a hundredth part of the first class. But the best class is in the 7th chapter of John: 'Out of his belly shall flow rivers of living water.' That is the kind of Christian we ought to be. . . .

"A great many think because they have been filled once, they are going to be full for all time after; but O, my friends, we are leaky vessels, and have to be kept right under the fountain all the time in order to keep full. If we are going to be used by God we have to be very humble. A man that lives close to God will be the humblest of men. I heard a man say that God always chooses the vessel that is close at hand. Let us keep near Him."

The service that succeeds, as illustrated in the life of D. L. Moody, was cogently summarized by the late Dr. C. L. Scofield, editor of the Scofield Reference Bible, who spoke at Moody's funeral service. In part he said:

"Doubtless this unlettered New England country boy became what he was by the grace of God. The secrets of Dwight L. Moody's power were: First, in a definite experience of Christ's saving grace. He has passed out of death into life, and he knew it. Secondly, he believed in the divine authority of the Scriptures. The Bible was to him the voice of God, and he made it resound as such in the consciences of men. Thirdly, he was baptized with the Holy Spirit, and he knew it. It was to him as definite an experience as his conversion. Fourthly, he was a man of prayer. He believed in a mighty and unfettered God. Fifthly, he believed in works, in ceaseless effort, in wise provision, in he power of organization, of publicity. He expected the supernatural to work, but through the natural. He hitched his wagon to a star, but he always kept the wheels on the ground and the axles well oiled."

And we of this generation who desire deeply and desperately that the Savior use us as He did Dwight Lyman Moody, must be both saved by grace and certain of our salvation; men both of faith and of the works that arise out of that faith; and servants who are both filled with the Spirit and overflowing therewith like rivers of living water.

Chapter Twelve

HANDLEY C. G. MOULE
The Fragrant Life

*G*od is no respecter of persons," declared Peter in the house of Cornelius, "but in every nation he that feareth him, and worketh righteousness, is accepted with him."

The life more abundant in Christ, the life that wins, is not restricted to any one group or denomination, to any one Christian creed or communion. To some it might seem strange to find Handley Moule, the late Bishop of Durham, listed among the Spirit-filled saints of the Most High who have come to know the living Lord through deep crises of consecration. In outward appearance this cultured son of Cambridge and of the Church of England, with resplendent episcopal robes befitting the station of one whose prerogatives included the right to stand at the right hand of the King of England at his coronation, was in direct contrast to his contemporary Dwight L. Moody in his customary business suit, or the rugged Finney in his rough homespun on the receding American frontier; yet all of them knew the enduement with power from on high.

Handley Moule completed his college training at Cambridge and had taught at the Marlborough School before he was truly converted to Christ. It was at Christmas time, 1866, that the twenty-five-year-old teacher, reared in a manse by godly parents, received the Savior for himself. In a letter written to his father the following February on the subject of ordination, he testified:

"My trust is that this very Christmas vacation, after a time of much mental wretchedness, I was able to find and to accept pardon and peace through the satisfaction of the Redeemer, as I had never done before; and to feel a truth and solid reality in the doctrine of the Cross as I have ever been taught it at home, such as I had sometimes painfully—very painfully—doubted of, under the continual droppings of the controversies and questions of the present day, and the differences, real and apparent, among Christians. In such an assured sight of the Savior as I then, I do trust, was permitted to have, I find now a comfort and hope even when at times faith and hope seem dying or (as it were) dead. . . . I mention all this very chiefly to ask for your prayers on such particular points for me; and to assure you that I am in a state, in spite of such confessions, *quite different,* as to repentance and faith and views of doctrine generally, to what I was a few months back; and also that I am finding in prayer and reading of the Bible quite a new strength and delight. . . ."

Academically thoroughly prepared, conservative in theology and evangelical outlook, godly and God fearing, gracious and gifted, Handley Moule seemed eminently qualified for the ministry. Despite the clear and unwavering assurance of faith in Christ, however, there lingered in his heart a yearning for a spiritual equipment and enduement that he could not quickly define. To his father he wrote: "But I sadly feel the need of tenfold grace before I can hope to be either a very happy Christian or—as a minister of Jesus Christ—a very useful one."

Four years after his ordination and entrance into the ministry as curate with his father, and while working on his Easter message, he wrote to a fellow minister as follows: ". . . oh, how dealing with such subjects brings me back on the view of my own native unbelief and hardness of heart. When shall I learn to live as in the presence of the risen and ever living Lord?"

At the time of his ordination, Moule's mother wrote to him that the burden of her prayer was that he might truly "receive the Holy Ghost for this office and work;" to which he had replied in part: "Oh, that I may soberly day by day review my vow on consecration, be humbled by it, and yet be made by it to feel a little more my hold on the Lord Jesus Christ."

The answer to his mother's prayer, and to his own longing, came years afterward. In 1882, during his third year of principalship at Ridley Hall, Moody and Sankey came to Cambridge. The university community was deeply stirred, as was the principal of Ridley Hall, who had been somewhat apprehensive that university men could not be reached by gospel preaching. In his diary for the first Monday night of the mission is the record: "Stayed to after meeting—first I had ever seen." For Friday he wrote: "University meeting, deeply solemn and full of blessing; gallery crowded afterwards with those who had received, or desired, blessing. . . ." On Sunday evening Principal Moule knelt beside Moody at the close of the service and heard the evangelist ask all who had received definite blessing at the meetings quietly to stand up while every eye was closed, and he heard Moody say under his breath as he saw the result: "My God, this is enough to live for."

The following year some "Keswick speakers" came to Cambridge with glowing testimony of the life of rest and victory in Christ. Principal Moule was still not satisfied in his own heart, and yet he was suspicious of the doctrinal soundness of "Keswick teaching." He knew that he needed deeper experience himself, yet he sought to content himself with criticism of the exegesis of Scripture made by Keswick leaders. With hunger of heart, however, he went to a Keswick convention the following year.

September 18, 1884, marked the great crisis in the life of Handley Moule. Afterward he made reference again and again to that date as a new departure in his life, a date when the reality and secret of a holy life became revealed to him.

The convention at Polmont was held in a great barn. Because of Moule's misgiving as to the soundness of the teaching he sat in the audience in a critical state of mind, but also with "hunger for some gracious thing, if it was to be found." A Christian businessman, William Sloan, spoke from Haggai 1:6, "Ye eat, but ye have not enough." Self, he pointed out, is the source of leanness in the soul. Then Evan H. Hopkins spoke, emphasizing that man, even an earnest Christian, cannot live in victory by his own merit and efforts but that what man cannot do the Spirit of God could accomplish in him. Observed Moule: "He piled up the promises of God to the soul that will do two things towards Him: surrender itself into His hands, and trust Him for His mighty victory within."

Just where he sat, Bishop Moule, the unsatisfied man of God, did two things; he yielded himself wholly and without reservation to the Savior as His bondslave, and he trusted definitely that the Lord Jesus would effect in him that transformation into His own image which the Lord alone can accomplish.

In his able and analytical exposition of *The Spiritual Unfolding of Bishop H. C. G. Moule,* John Baird summarizes excellently the transformation that then transpired. "Before the meeting was over he yielded himself to his Redeemer, accepting His word that He would fulfill all He had undertaken in His promises to do. It was a swift act of self-determination. He was convicted rather than startled. He swung open the doors of his heart in his welcome to Jesus to be evermore his Lord. A great inflow of feeling followed. All slackness was ended. His spirit rose under an access of welcome relief. He found comfort in the thought that he was now in the keeping of a gracious Redeemer. He entered into abundance of blessing and fullness of life. It was life indeed—not life merely endured, nor life as a task, nor life as a struggle—but life as a joy and a victory with the spiritual forces of the soul undivided.

"The all sufficiency of Jesus for sanctification was the vivifying truth. Depressed by a feeling of his limitation—conscious he was marred by a self not wholly subdued—this new aspect flashed upon him with illuminating power. He had felt holiness to be a vain endeavour in his own strength. But Christian hope took on a troubled sea, as he felt himself swept with willing mind into prompt and exulting acceptance. Sweet is the dawn of light and day but even more so is the dawn of enriching experience.

"Such is the record of the hour and opportunity of the great self-dedication which came to him as he rose to this new zone of thought. It was never regretted and it was never undone. Rather, it was repeated and reconfirmed day by day. It was his testimony in after years that the trust he reposed in Jesus had been abundantly honoured and satisfied. If self-will is the sum of moral evil, engagement with Christ to be his in a whole-hearted way, is the sum of moral good. Moule felt the thrill of putting all things aside for Him."

Dr. Moule was constrained to write and to tell the wonderful reality of his experience in Christ. He said, "If a reference to personal experience may be permitted, I may indeed here 'set my seal.' Never shall I forget the gain to conscious faith and peace which came to my own soul, not long after a first decisive and appropriating view of the crucified Lord as the sinner's sacrifice of peace, from a more intelligent and conscious hold upon the living and most gracious personality of the Spirit through whose mercy the soul had got that blessed view. It was a new development of insight into the love of God. *It was a new contact as it were with the inner and eternal movements of redeeming goodness and power,* a new discovery in divine resources."

The lasting results of the dawning of the new day are to be observed in the every widening spiritual influence of God's servant. The enrollment at Ridley Hall was augmented, and with the increase there came problems that were triumphantly faced and overcome in the power of the new life. In the principalship that continued until 1899, and in the nineteen years of his bishopric he was ever an earnest and faithful counselor to clergymen, especially to the younger men who were drawn to him, and to the laity. Out of a quickened mind and a burning heart he wrote voluminously, and with great blessing, and in the pulpit his message was always filled with the Lord Jesus Christ, His Person and His work.

The "life that is Christ" knows no bounds of ecclesiastical preferment or denominational preference, and while Bishop Moule remained always a staunch Anglican he had the widest possible fellowship with every fellow believer in the Lord Jesus.

He was, therefore, a living example of the Keswick motto: "All one in Christ." The Keswick message of the union of the believer with the Savior and the unity of the body of Christ he expressed by life and by lip during the thirty-six years that extended from his full committal to Christ until the close of his life. That message and the life of the messenger were adequately and eloquently expressed on the occasion of his last visit to Keswick in 1919. The messages given on that occasion were published in book form under the title *Christ and the Christian.*

In the first message he stated: "I know not how better to give in its vital essence the Keswick message than in the words of M'Cheyne: 'Christ *for* us is all our righteousness before a holy God; Christ *in* us is all our strength in an ungodly world.' The first limb of the statement refers rather to what Keswick takes for granted than what it distinctively teaches. . . . The distinctive message of our Convention is that which speaks itself out in the second limb of M'Cheyne's pregnant saying: 'Christ *in* us is all our strength in an ungodly world.' So the young Scottish prophet wrote, a long generation before our convention arose.... The God-given work of Keswick, for it was indeed God-given, was only to emphasize with a new accent of decision this wonderful but authentic and orthodox gospel for the inner life."

And what was the open secret of the saint in surplice? It was simply this, he said, "Holiness by Faith, a life humbly true to God, made possible, made actual, by the use, for victory, of the trusted Christ within." Bishop Moule could underline as his own the experience of the apostle Paul: "But thanks be unto God, who always leadeth us in triumph in Christ, and makest manifest through us the savor of his knowledge in every place. For we are a sweet savor of Christ unto God, in them that are saved, and in them that perish; to the one a savor from death unto death; to the other a savor from life unto life. . . ." (2 Cor. 2:14, 15 ASV).

Chapter Thirteen

ANDREW MURRAY
The Abiding Life

It was in the last moments of the Last Supper, with all their tenderness, that the Savior taught His disciples, and us through them, that "I am the vine, ye are the branches: He that abideth in me, and I in him, the same bringeth forth much fruit: for without me ye can do nothing" (John 15:5).

Ever since that momentous truth was declared to the disciples, faithful and devout followers of the Lord Jesus have found experientially its glorious reality. Illustrative of this life is Andrew Murray of South Africa.

For nearly one hundred years his has been a household name among earnest Christians who have yearned for the abiding life; and through his preaching or his pen many have come to its realization. The latter part of the nineteenth century and the first part of the twentieth knew him as a man of believing prayer, a preacher of the whole counsel of God, a Bible conference leader and a voluminous author. His writings are still in great demand because they continue to meet a real need in the hearts of God's people.

A vivid description of the quiet-spoken and deeply effective man of God has been left to us. It was said of him that Andrew Murray desired to be known as a Christian, simply as a follower of Jesus, and that he seemed to examine everyone he met for the Christian element in him. "His keen, yearning look" wrote an observer, "appears to scan the face of his interlocutor for the witness of the Christ-life there, and to plead above all things for loyalty to the one Master. You cannot help saying to yourself, 'This man wants me to belong to Jesus Christ.' No one who has talked with him, even on casual themes, can forget that wistful glance."

The observation continued: "He is, I suppose, well known to most readers of religious literature by his devotional books, notably *Abide in Christ*. His nature is profoundly devotional; he carries with him the atmosphere of prayer. He seems always wrapped about with a mantle of adoration. When preaching or conducting a service, his whole being is thrown into the task, and he glows with a fervency of spirit which it seems impossible for human flesh to sustain. At times he startles and overwhelms the listeners. Earnestness and power of the electric sort stream from him, and affect alike the large audience or the quiet circle gathered round him. In his slight, spent frame, of middle height, he carries in repose a volcanic energy which, when he is roused, bursts its barriers and sweeps all before it. Then his form quivers and dilates, the lips tremble, the features work, the eyes spasmodically open and close, as from the white-hot furnace of his spirit he pours the molten torrent of his unstudied eloquence. The thin face and almost emaciated body are transfigured and illumined. The staid, venerable minister of the nineteenth century, with the sober, clerical garb and stiff white tie, which is *de rigueur* among the Dutch clergy, disappears, and an old Hebrew prophet stands before us—another Isaiah with his glowing imagery, a second Hosea with his plaintive, yearning appeals, Audiences bend before the seeping rain of his words like willows before a gale. The heart within the hearer is bowed, and the intellect awed. . . ."

No truth of God can be written larger than that the crisis of the deeper life, like that of regeneration, follows no fixed pattern. As the wind "bloweth where it listeth," so the Spirit moves as He will. Andrew Murray exemplifies excellently the reality of the Spirit-filled life that derives its reality from the Person of the Holy Spirit, wholly apart from any dynamic emotional experience. The man of God can best tell his own testimony, as related by himself at the English Keswick:

"Some of you have heard," said Andrew Murray, "how I have pressed upon you the two stages in the Christian life, and the step from the one to the other. The first ten years of my spiritual life were manifestly spent on the lower stage. I was a minister, I may say, as zealous and as earnest and as happy in my work as anyone, as far as love of the work was concerned. Yet, all the time, there was burning in my heart a dissatisfaction and restlessness inexpressible. What the reason? I had never learnt with all my theology that obedience was possible. My justification was as clear as noonday. I knew the hour in which I received from God the joy of pardon. I remember in my little room at Bloemfontein how I used to sit and think, What is the matter? Here I am, knowing that God has justified me in the blood of Christ, but I have no power for service. My thoughts, my words, my actions, my unfaithfulness—everything troubled me. Though all around thought me one of the most earnest of men, my life was one of deep dissatisfaction. I struggled and prayed as best I could."

Murray continued: "One day I was talking with a missionary. I do not think that he knew much of the power of sanctification himself—he would have admitted it. When we were talking and he saw my earnestness he said, 'Brother, remember that when God puts a desire into your heart, He will fulfill it.'" That helped me; I thought of it a hundred times. I want to say the same to you, who are plunging about and struggling in the quagmire of helplessness and doubt. The desire that God puts into your heart He will fulfill. . . .

"Well, God helped me, and for seven or eight years I went on, always enquiring and seeking, and always getting. Then came, about 1870, the great Holiness Movement. The letters that appeared in *The Revival* (now *The Christian*) touched my heart; and I was in close fellowship with what took place at Oxford and Brighton, and it all helped me. Perhaps if I were to talk of consecration I might tell you of an evening there in my own study in Cape Town. Yet I cannot say that that was my deliverance, for I was still struggling. Later on, my mind became much exercised about the baptism of the Holy Spirit, and I gave myself to God as perfectly as I could to receive the baptism of the Spirit. Yet there was failure; God forgive it. It was somehow as if I could not get what I wanted. Through all these stumblings God led me, without any very special experience that I can point to; but as I look back I do believe now that He was giving me more and more of His blessed Spirit, had I but known it better.

"I can help you more, perhaps, by speaking, not of any marked experience, but by telling very simply what I think God has given me now, in contrast to the first ten years of my Christian life. In the first place, I have learnt to place myself before God every day, as a vessel to be filled with His Holy Spirit. He has filled me with the blessed assurance that He, as the everlasting God, has guaranteed His work in me. If there is one lesson that I am learning day by day, it is this: that it is God who worketh all in all. Oh, that I could help any brother or sister to realize this! . . .

"You will ask me," Murray said, "are you satisfied? Have you got all you want? God forbid. With the deepest feeling of my soul I can say that I am satisfied with Jesus now; but there is also the consciousness of how much fuller the revelation can be of the exceeding abundance of His grace. Let us never hesitate to say, This is only the beginning. When we are brought into the holiest of all, we are only beginning to take our right position with the Father."

No power; then because of utter heart surrender on Andrew Murray's part, the Almighty took over his life.

No fruitfulness; then Murray learned to abide in the Vine, by implicit obedience and not by fluctuating feelings.

No satisfaction; then he learned that the Holy One "satisfieth the longing soul and filleth the hungry soul with goodness."

Andrew Murray knew for himself the Spirit-filled life and his life encouraged others to know this way of peace and power for themselves. Amy Carmichael in *Though the Mountains Shake* tells of an experience in 1895 when Andrew Murray of South Africa was in England taking part in various conventions, and because of a physical breakdown in Japan she had returned home. At one time they were both guests in the same house. "I knew that his books were very good," she said. "Not that I had read one of them, but a neat row of them, dressed in sober grey, lived in my mother's room, and she and everybody said how good they were." Amy Carmichael wondered if he was as good as his books, and found that he was even better. "For," she said, "there was not only goodness, there was a delicious dry humor, dauntless courage, and the gentleness and simplicity of a dear child. And he was very loving. He never seemed to be tired of loving."

Then something painful happened to Mr. Murray, Miss Carmichael records that this is how he met it.

"He was quiet for a while with his Lord, then he wrote these words for himself:

"First, he brought me here, it is by His will I am in this strait place: in that fact I will rest.

Next, he will keep me here in His love, and give me grace to behave as His child.

Then, He will make the trial a blessing, teaching me the lessons He intends me to learn, and working in me the grace He means to bestow.

Last, in his good time He can bring me out again—how and when He knows.

Let me say I am here,

(1) By God's appointment,
(2) In His keeping,
(3) Under His training,
(4) For His time."

Such a story is timeless. Many have been helped by it, not once only, but often.

From Andrew Murray's *The Secret of Adoration* comes this exhortation: "Take time. Give God time to reveal Himself to you. Give yourself time to be silent and quiet before Him, waiting to receive, through the Spirit, the assurance of His presence with you, His power working in you. Take time to read His Word as in His presence, that from it you may know what He asks of you and what He promises you. Let the Word create around you, create within you a holy atmosphere, a holy heavenly light, in which your soul will be refreshed and strengthened for the work of daily life."

Such indeed is the abiding life that draws its sustenance and strength from the Vine. By the refreshing and reviving flow of the Holy Spirit through that life there is prayer that prevails, preaching that is powerful, love that is contagious, joy that overflows, and peace that passes understanding. It is the adoration that is stillness to know God for one's self. It is the obedience that does the Savior's bidding in the light of the Word. It is the fruitfulness that arises spontaneously from abiding in the Vine.

Chapter Fourteen

ROBERT E. NICHOLAS

The Satisfying Life

The first reference in the Bible to Christian businessmen is found in Acts, chapter 6. They were "men of honest report, full of the Holy Ghost and wisdom."

The first seven deacons, appointed by the apostles, were businessmen, not preachers. Their responsibility was to look out for the welfare of widows and orphans, and to that end they had to keep accounts, make purchases, handle inventories, and make distribution according to need.

In addition to integrity, intelligence, and good reputation, the one prime requirement for the man chosen for this service was fullness of the Holy Spirit. "Be filled with the Sprit" was and is an injunction for all Christians, be they manufacturers or merchants, coal miners or ministers of the gospel.

By the indwelling Holy Spirit the life of the Lord Jesus is made manifest, and only thus can the businessman "Be kindly affectioned one to another with brotherly love.... Not slothful in business; fervent in Spirit; serving the Lord" (Rom. 12:10, 11). Williams translates that phrase: *always on fire with the Spirit.*

It is interesting indeed that there was a first-century Nicholas who, filled with the Holy Spirit, was a good businessman for God on behalf of his fellow Christians, and that there is a twentieth-century Nicholas who found the same enduement of the Holy Spirit absolutely essential for effective service and stewardship.

Robert E. Nicholas, who was an Oak park, Illinois, "elder statesman" among businessmen, was born on a farm in Caledonia, Ontario, Canada in 1882, the eldest son in a large family of boys and girls. His parents, Gideon and Elizabeth Nicholas, were earnest Christians who reared their family in the wholesome disciplines of the Holy Bible and hard work. In the local Methodist church the children learned the way of salvation and the joy of Christian service.

There was no promising future for the farm lad in his home area so at the age of nineteen Robert Nicholas went to Chicago to find employment. Work was not plentiful in those days nor could the wages be termed decidedly attractive. But in what was to him a clear leading of the Holy Spirit he found work in a Chicago hardware store, whereby diligence and duty over long hours of every weekday he found favor with his employers and advancement came rapidly.

His father on the Ontario farm was pleased, but also a bit disturbed, to learn that his lad was receiving the munificent wages of a dollar a day—six dollars for a week of sixty hours' work. As a result, his first letter contained much advice to his son, and included Solomon's searching proverb: "There is that scattereth, and yet increaseth; and there is that withholdeth more than is meet, but it tendeth to poverty" (11:24).

Thus the young clerk was reminded anew of the principle of consistent and proportionate stewardship such as he had seen in the home in Ontario, and he carefully tithed his weekly wages. The remainder of his six dollars a week was needed for room rent and the small allowance for each day's meals, with very little, if any, left for a "treat."

Robert Nicholas, alone in a large city and far from home, did not forget his mother's God and his father's faith; rather, he at once identified himself with an active Methodist church. Weekends found him busy in Sunday school, in Epworth

League meetings, and witnessing for the Savior. Among the young people in Christian circles he met many new friends, especially one lovely lassie from the Lakeview Mission Covenant Church on the north side of Chicago, who moved over to the Methodist church, and became Mrs. Nicholas.

Five years after coming to Chicago, and largely on borrowed capital, Mr. Nicholas established his own hardware business in nearby Oak Park. With good business foresight he saw possibilities in that expanding village; and with business acumen and executive ability, along with plenty of hard work, he built that first store into one of the largest retail hardware, house furnishing and appliance businesses in the State of Illinois. In time, as a leading businessman in Oak Park, he was the inspiration and leader in the development of the Lake Marion business district, which is now the commercial center of the city. He was instrumental in bringing branches of the large department stores in the Chicago "Loop" out to Oak Park.

But the heart of this merchant was not satisfied. Although his business was progressing steadily and he and his wife were happy with their well-established family (there were three little children), he felt there was something lacking. The Almighty, who alone can satisfy the longing soul and fill the hungry soul with goodness, was leading His servant in ways past finding out, that he might know the fullness of the Holy Spirit in his life.

It was late summer, 1914. Canada sprang to the side of England when Belgium was invaded by Germany. The war brought problems to Canadian families. From a sister living in Saskatchewan Mr. Nicholas received a wire saying that he was urgently needed there. His first reaction was, "I cannot possibly go. I am burdened with my work and business appointments, and with responsibilities to my family and local church." It appeared from every angle to be a most unfortunate time. In looking to the Lord, however, his own immediate problems seemed to resolve themselves and the next day he was on his way to western Canada.

One clear truth stands out in the subsequent events of that journey. When God has an appointment for you, you are not going to miss it! And God had an appointment for R. E. Nicholas.

It seemed that he almost missed it. There in that little Saskatchewan town Mr. Nicholas left the home of his sister one day to drive out across the plains to visit another sister some five miles away. Now the west wind does on occasion blow with considerable vehemence across those great wheat lands, but not often to the extent of deterring a sturdy Model T operated by a determined driver. But on this particular day "R. E.," as he was called, had not gone more than two miles when he found he could not force that Ford any farther against the wind. Turning it around on the dirt road he found to his amazement that it ran perfectly when going in the direction of town. Several times he turned it around and tried to head toward the farm, only to be entirely unsuccessful.

God was in those circumstances.

On reaching his sister's home again, he was introduced to an evangelist who had come for a brief visit that afternoon. This preacher was holding services in the village. After the word of introduction, he inquired, "Mr. Nicholas, have you given your life completely to God?" So earnest and effective was the inquiry that Mr. Nicholas fell at once to his knees in prayer, as though he were pressed down by someone. His heart was smitten with the conviction that he should consecrate himself wholly to the Lord; but as he prayed he seemed to get no response from heaven, nor relief of spirit.

After that prayer session with God's servant, and some instruction in the Scriptures, Mr. Nicholas promised to attend the evening service. True to his word he went to the meeting determined to yield his life fully to the Lord. What that yielding might mean he did not know, nor did he concern himself with the outcome of it.

When the altar call was given for those who would surrender completely to the Lord, he went forward, and knelt down to pray. As he recalled later, it seemed to him at that moment that all the forces of Satan were attacking him, and "I experienced," he said, "such blackness of opposition as I had never known up to that time."

With greater earnestness than he had ever known, he prayed. Others joined with him in prayer at the altar. "So far as I knew and understood," he says, "I yielded my life without reservation to God. Finally, as I prayed, I began to praise God; then the Holy Spirit filled my heart until I could not contain the joy that came to me as I continued to praise my Lord.

"I arose from that altar of prayer a new man and my life, notwithstanding my failures and shortcomings, has never been the same since that meeting with God. Over the years there has been tremendous pressure of business and large responsibilities in the community and in the church, and these very pressures might have drawn me away from the Savior but for the fact that there was always the knowledge of the indwelling Spirit who had come to abide in my heart."

At once the faithful Holy Spirit, who filled to overflowing the life of this young and aggressive merchant, began to show him His faithfulness. The problems of his relatives were satisfactorily settled and he boarded the train for home. "I was so filled with praise and rejoicing," he recalls, "that sometimes I left my seat and went out in the vestibule of the railroad car where I might praise God aloud. I knew that there was indeed a peace that passes understanding, love that passes knowledge, and a joy that abounds."

In order to reach home by Sunday evening, Mr. Nicholas was counting on a train connection in Minneapolis, but the train from western Canada was so late that the Chicago train departed before they arrived. He was not only very disappointed, he was also much perplexed. There was no train until evening, and he knew no one in Minneapolis. He set out to find a church in which to hear the Word of God. Before long he passed a large, imposing church, but it occurred to him that quite possibly he might find warmer fellowship in a smaller church. For an hour or more he continued walking without finding such a church; rather, he found himself again in front of that same large church.

It was time for the morning service, and the stranger from Chicago entered the house of God. That morning the pastor, the late Dr. W. B. Riley of First Baptist Church, Minneapolis, who was unknown to Mr. Nicholas at that time, preached a wonderful sermon on the Second Coming of Christ, a doctrine about which Mr. Nicholas knew little. "I realized," said R. E., "how hungry I was to hear about the return of the Lord Jesus, now that I had dedicated my life fully to Him."

Then it was that Mr. Nicholas understood why the Highest had hindered his making that close train connection for home. From that first experience he began to learn indeed that "our disappointments are God's appointments," and that the Holy Spirit can guide by a closed door as well as one that is open.

When he arrived home the following morning, Mrs. Nicholas was busy in the basement with the laundry. As her husband came down the stairs, her first word was, "Rob, what has happened to you?"

There was no need for the hurried, and often harried, hardware merchant to call attention to his experience of being filled with the Spirit. His very countenance and presence showed forth the reality of the indwelling Savior. His response was given in a few words of personal testimony, with tears. There by the laundry tubs Mr. Nicholas and his wife knelt together, and there she made that same consecration to the Lord Jesus and realized the fullness of His Spirit.

The outreach of that crisis of the deeper life is difficult to measure. The hardware business, as has been stated, expanded rapidly to become one of the largest in metropolitan Chicago and throughout the State of Illinois. It was sold in 1929, and Mr. Nicholas turned his ability and experience into other commercial enterprises in Oak Park and its environs. For ten years he was president of a building and loan association that went through the dark and difficult days of the depression without a single default. Homes were saved for owners who were in straitened circumstances, and many can recall with gratitude the counsel, patience, and, if necessary, rebuke on the part of the conscientious association president.

His deep interest in Christian young people and his desire for their thorough preparation for whatever service God may have for them in the ministry, whether it be on the mission field, in the schoolroom, or in the store, led him to accept trusteeship in Moody Bible Institute and at Wheaton College. In this capacity he has been always a constructive, consistent, spiritually-minded counselor and helper.

Robert Nicholas would be the last one to speak of his service and his stewardship for the Savior. Missionaries and mission boards, his church and philanthropic enterprises in Oak Park and elsewhere, schools and students, far and near, have been helped by him, usually anonymously.

And so, as one of God's choicest businessmen looks back over the years, and especially to the crisis that brought him to the knowledge of God's Holy Spirit, he says: "By this experience, and by others which have followed, my life has been changed from that of a nominal Christian to one with purpose and convictions. There has been an abiding sense of the Holy Spirit's presence in my life. He has given me an appetite for the things of God and an appreciation of the Scriptures. In answer to prayer he has given me ability in business, strength under strain, confidence and courage.

"I can understand," he says, "why so many Christians do not have the joy they might have, or do not have overflowing praise in their heart. There must be a full surrender of life to the Savior to have the fullness of the Holy Spirit—'For it is God which worketh in you both to will and to do of his good pleasure' (Philippians 2:13)."

Such is the testimony of R. E. Nicholas to the indwelling Spirit of God, the source and wellspring of his full and abundant life.

Chapter Fifteen

WILLIAM P. NICHOLSON
The Soul-Winning Life

*T*he career and Christian service of William P. Nicholson, the Irish evangelist, can be accurately summarized in the expression: From sea fever to soul-winning!

Born in county Down near Bangor, in North Ireland, he seemed destined to follow the sea. His father was a sea captain in the golden age of sailing ships during the second half of the nineteenth century, and he took his laddie for his first voyage when the latter was only six years of age. To this day, Nicholson has a painting of his father's barque, *The Muriel*, fully rigged, with every sail set; and although the evangelist is now in his eighties, sea fever rises deep within him as he contemplates that ship. Could it be that far distant in his background is the heritage of the Vikings, those restless, fearless, sea raiders who ravaged the coasts of Ireland in medieval times? Could be.

School books and commonplace employment on the land had no place in young William's thinking; so at fifteen he sailed away from home as an apprentice seaman. He recalls:

"It was a hard and harsh training. It either made you or broke you. Yet I loved it, especially up aloft during the gale of wind—the wind shrieking through the rigging, and the ship rolling from side to side, the seas like miniature mountains. It intoxicated me. Food was scarce—tough salt beef and salt pork and Liverpool pantiles for biscuits. The regular hours, fresh air and hard work, and instant obedience made you healthy, if mostly unhappy."

But the Irish sailor lad was taken from the sea to become a fisher of men as dramatically, if not more so, than was Peter of Bethsaida long ago. On one voyage with a cargo of coal, the ship on which he sailed ran into a terrific northeaster in the "roaring forties" after rounding Cape Horn. In the tempest the ship tossed and rolled as if it would go under, and the cargo began to shift. With mast broken and sails in wreckage there seemed to be no hope. By morning, another sailing ship came near; but the half-frozen men on Nicholson's ship did not dare jump into the sea because they knew they could never reach the lifeboat. Thereupon, the other ship sailed away and left them to their doom.

The crew, however, was able to break into the hold and shift the cargo until the ship righted itself. With what rigging was left they were able to turn back around Cape Horn and reached the Falkland Islands.

The cry to God for mercy made by the crew members, including Nicholson, when in their extremity, meant nothing to them once they were again in safety. Snatched from the sea, but not saved!

After completing his apprenticeship and working for some time on railroad construction in South Africa, he returned home. It was there by the fireside on the morning of May 22, 1899, that he was snatched the second time "from the sea"; and that time he was really saved. While reading the morning paper and smoking and awaiting the breakfast being prepared by his godly mother, he heard suddenly, and without warning, a voice saying, "Now or never. You must decide to accept or to reject Christ." In that moment, trembling with fear, he cried out, "Lord, I yield. I repent of all my sin and now accept Thee as my Savior."

He recalls, "Suddenly and powerfully and consciously, I was saved. Such a peace and freedom from fear, such a sweet and sure assurance filled my soul. I turned to my mother and said, 'Mother, I am saved.' She looked at me and nearly collapsed, and said, 'When?' I said, 'Just now.' 'Where?' 'Here, where I am sitting.' She cried with joy unspeakable. She couldn't say a word, but just hugged me and cried."

William Nicholson had been saved, and he knew it. "I have never had any doubts about my salvation," he declares. "The Blood had been applied and the Spirit answered to the Blood. I never doubted about my dear mother's word about my natural birth, and do you think it's strange of me to take God's word without a doubt or fear? I became a new creature, and began hating sin. I tried hard to love God, the Bible, the church, and prayer; but what a failure I made of it."

The crisis of the deeper life, with the enduement of the Holy Spirit for service, came to young Nicholson a few months after his conversion. It is best to let an Irishman tell his own story, so here it is.

"The peace and joy and assurance continued, but in a fluctuating way. Sometimes doubting, sometimes trusting, sometimes joyful, sometimes sad. All grosser sins dropped off me, and I had no sorrow about it, or any bother with them; but the sins of the flesh and the spirit continued to plague me greatly: envy, jealousy, malice, hatred. I could crush them down, but they continued to rise up again, more vigorous than ever.

"The fear of man was a dreadful snare, and I was helplessly caught by it. I was ashamed of Christ, and ashamed of being seen with out-and-out Christians. I was a sneak and a coward, if ever there was one. I despised myself, but was helpless about it. . . .

"I attended church twice every Sunday, and joined the men's Bible class. I read my Bible but didn't get any good out of it, and had little or no desire for it. Prayer was a real penance, and seemingly useless. What a wretched, miserable experience I was passing through!

"I lived in this distracted state for nearly seven months after my conversion. Some have told me I wasn't converted at all—that I only thought I was. But they were wrong. I was truly born again, and a new creature in Jesus Christ. I had the inward witness clear, and the outward evidence that I was a changed man. . . . I hated sin, but was continually overcome by it. I loved holiness, and longed to be perfectly whole, but never experienced it. I was truly a child of God, but a slave of the devil. My life was up and down, but more down than up. I was committing sin and confessing it, but rarely having victory over it. I believed there was deliverance for me, but how to obtain it I didn't know.

"I knew some Christians who were living a victorious, joyous, soul-winning life. How I envied them! I am sure if I had only made known to them the fluctuating, failing kind of life I was living, they would have led me into the open secret; but I was ashamed to make my experience known. . . .

"Thank God, the day of my deliverance was at hand. One of the leading businessmen of the town, an out-and-out man for Christ and souls, arranged for a 'Convention for the Deepening of the Christian Life.' My older brother, James, and a close friend of his in his student days, Reverend J. Stuart Holden, were the convention leaders.

"If they had called the conference 'holiness meetings' I would have been frightened, and would never have attended. I would have called them wild fire and fanaticism; and being a good well-behaved, blue-stockinged Presbyterian, I would have shunned them.

"From the very first sermon I heard, I was sure my brother had told Holden about me, for he made public my miserable condition. It made me feel clean mad! I determined I would not go to another service; but I was there the next night. I was more sure than ever that my brother had put the preacher up to preach at me. I became more angry every night, but could not keep myself from attendance.

"Stuart Holden made the secret of the victorious Christian life so clear and plain. After one has been born again by the Spirit of God he can live victoriously only by the Holy Spirit. I began to understand that I could not attain this life by self effort or ceremonies, for it was 'not by might nor by power, but by the Spirit.' It was not an *attainment,* but an *obtainment.* Christ was God's unspeakable gift to the world. The Holy Spirit was Christ's gift to His church. I had been trying to do what the Holy Spirit *alone* could, and would, do for me. But I must receive Him by faith, on the ground of grace, and He would sanctify my heart, and apply the Blood, thus cleansing me from all sin and making the victory purchased by Christ on Calvary experiential. As I walked in the light as He was in the light, He would maintain the life of holiness and victory in my life day by day.

"It was all so wonderful and new to me. I had never heard such truth before. Oh, how my heart ached for just such a life, but I was hindered by fear of the consequences. I didn't want to be anything or do anything a Presbyterian ought not to be or do. I tried so hard to make the Lord see and understand my fears and feelings, but He had no sympathy for my fears. I couldn't make Him a Presbyterian!

"The Salvation Army had come to our town. The Corps was composed of two wee girls in uniform. They held open-air meetings and made a noise with their tambourines. Their first soldier was a man called Daft Jimmy. He had hardly enough brains to give him a headache, but he had sense enough to get saved. He carried the flag as they marched the streets. On his jersey, a red one, he had the women put with white yarn these words on his back, 'Saved from public opinion.'

"I was told by Satan that I would have to go to the open-air meeting and march down the street with two wee girls and a fool. Maybe that didn't fill me with horrible dread! I would be laughed at by all my friends. I would lose my reputation.

"I said, 'Lord, I will be willing to go to Timbuctoo or Hong King, or even die recently as a martyr.' I couldn't get out of it. I became more and more miserable and, oh, so hungry for freedom and victory.

"At last I became desperate. The last night of the convention I saw it was a clean-cut, unconditional surrender; or continued wandering in failure, defeat and dissatisfaction. I left the meeting and went down to the shore, and there under a clear sky and shining stars I made the complete unconditional surrender. I cried out, 'Come in. Come in, Holy Spirit. Thy work of great blessing begin. By faith I lay hold of the promise, and claim complete victory over sin.'

"Hallelujah! What a thrill, what a peace, what a joy! Although an old-fashioned Presbyterian I began to weep and sing and rejoice like an old-fashioned Free Methodist. When I came home, I told my mother, 'the surrender has been made, and I am free and so happy.' She was delighted, for she told me she wondered whether I was really saved or not. She knew the blessing, for she had received it under the Rev. Andrew Murray's preaching held in a convention in Belfast. The wonder to me was that all of the fear of what men might say or do had vanished, and now I was willing to do anything or go anywhere. The very thing I dreaded most before receiving the blessing, about the Salvation Army meeting, was faced. I couldn't say I was very happy about it; but I told the Lord I would do what He wanted, cost what it may. So I went to the open-air meeting on a Saturday night. . . .

"As I walked down the street that Saturday it seemed as if every friend and relative I ever had were out and about. When

I came to the open-air meeting and saw the two wee Salvation Army girls singing and rattling their tambourines, and poor Daft Jimmy holding the flag, I nearly turned back. Talk about dying! I was dying hard that night. I stepped off the footpath, and stood in the ring. The soldier looked at me. Then to my horror one of them said, 'The people don't stop and listen: let us get down on our knees and pray.' What could I do? I couldn't run away. So down I got on my knees.

"The crowd gathered around. I could hear their laughter and jeers. The officer prayed a telegram prayer—short and to the point. I could have wished the prayer had been as long as the 119th Psalm. I stood up, blushing and nervous. They got the collection while the crowd was there, and then to my horror, she said, 'Brother! take this tambourine and lead the march down the street to the Barracks.' I couldn't let a girl beat me, so I took it. That did it. My shackles fell off, and I was free; my fears all gone.

"I started down the street, whether in the body or out of the body, I can't tell. I lost my reputation, and fear of man: joy and peace and glory filled me. I can see now, and understand why the Lord dealt with me so drastically. I would never, I believe, have come right through and out-and-out for Christ, in any other way. I was naturally timid and shy. I lost something that night I never want to find again, and I found something I never want to lose. That is, I lost my reputation and fear of man, and found the joy and peace of the overflowing fullness of the Spirit. Hallelujah!"

On street corners and in cottages, in the city and in the villages, in his place of employment on the railroad and in the churches, Nicholson became a fearless and flaming winner of souls. Because of his enthusiasm and effectiveness he was advised by earnest friends to prepare for Christian work. His new friend, Stuart Holden, advised him not to be in a hurry;

rather, to wait on God until a door for Bible preparation would be opened.

A glimpse of his service in those days is this reminiscence: "Every Sunday I held a meeting in a wee Orange Hall in a village a few miles from Bangor. I visited every home every Sunday before the service, inviting them to come to my meeting. I prayed with everyone who would allow me, and left a Spurgeon sermon. One dear old lady sitting at the door of her thatched cottage, when asked to come to my service, said, 'God love you, Mr. Nicholson, I don't need to go because you speak so loud the whole village can hear you.' My seafaring life gave me a good voice, so when I got warmed up preaching, you could hear me a mile away or more."

In His own way and time the Almighty led His young servant to the Bible Training Institute in Glasgow. Under godly and gifted instructors he was taught the wonders of the Scriptures. The Bible became his only textbook, and witnessing for the Savior and winning souls his greatest delight. After Bible School days he became an evangelist for the Lanarkshire Christian Union, an interdenominational society of leading Christian businessmen in that part of Scotland. Evangelistic services were held in the coal mining villages during the winter, and tent campaigns were held in the summertime. There the Lord gave him great favor among the people. Many came to a saving knowledge of the Lord Jesus, and many yielded themselves fully to the Savior and became Spirit-filled, soul-saving Christians.

Some of his early experiences in evangelism must be preserved for posterity. He recalls:

"During the summer we held our missions in a big tent. At one place, while erecting the tent, a big strong miner came and helped me to get the tent up. He held the pegs while I hammered them in with a 14 lb. hammer. It was sunny and hot, and I was wearing dungarees and singlet. The man said, 'The way you are working would put to shame the preacher. I suppose Nicholson will come all dressed up and begin preaching after you have done all the hard work.' I never let on who I was, but let him talk away about the well-fed, fat, lazy preacher. He would do no good, he said; and for his own part, the miner wouldn't come near a meeting! I didn't contradict him.

"Our first meeting was held on the next Sunday afternoon. When I reached the platform, whom should I see buy my good helper. I looked at him, and he gazed at me. He evidently couldn't believe I was the man he helped put up the tent. I worked hard getting the meeting into a good, happy swing, ready for the preaching. When giving the announcements, and telling who I was, I said, 'I have something good to tell you about the erecting of the tent.' I told them about the man who helped me, and what he said about me, and added that best of all he was there in the tent! I didn't expose him, but most of the audience knew him for a notable sinner. Maybe they didn't laugh! Best of all, he was soundly converted."

One more Nicholson recollection from those early days of evangelism must be included:

"What prayer meetings we used to have—all nights and half nights of prayer. The noise at times was intreating and joyful. The way some prayed, you would have thought God was a million miles away, or deaf. One night when a big-voiced man was praying, one of the nice, timid, quiety prayer warriors tugged at his coat and said, 'Brother, God isn't deaf.' 'No,' said the man. 'God isn't deaf, but these sinners seem to be.'

"One prayed, 'Lord, give me a good reputation in hell and with the old devil.' He created a laugh. Afterwards, I took him aside and said that he shouldn't say things at prayer to cause us to laugh. He said, 'Mr. Nicholson, I didn't say it that way. I had been reading it in the Bible,' I asked, 'Where?' He turned to Acts 19:13–15 where it is recounted that the seven sons of Sceva, exorcists, called over those possessed with demons, 'We adjure you by Jesus whom Paul preacheth,' and were answered by the evil spirit, 'Jesus I know, and Paul I know; but who are ye?' He said, 'I want the devil to know who I am.' I couldn't say a word. He was a new convert, and had been a great sinner.

"Those were great days, and great victories were won. We always managed a riot or a revival. Sometimes a riot and no revival, but never a revival without a riot!"

After training and testing days were over, God's servant was called to assist the late Dr. Wilbur Chapman and Charles M. Alexander in their evangelistic campaign the world over. The Irish evangelist sailed for Melbourne, Australia, in March 1909, for the campaign "Down Under."

Glorious days of revival there were but the beginning for him; and following the decades he journeyed around the world more than ten times, and witnessed for the Savior in nearly every land on the face of the earth. Tens of thousands came to the Savior in his evangelistic preaching, and countless Christians came to know for themselves the Spirit-filled life. The extent of such service will be made known only in eternity. Who can judge the impact of the lives whom God's servant has led to the Savior?

An illustration will suffice. On Sunday morning, September 23, 1923, a young upstart, unsaved, sophisticated, and self-confident, came to the Savior. He was a stranger to any church in Los Angeles; but in his brief stay there had attended a dance every night. One Sunday he thought it would be nice to go to church, to keep up the spiritual side of his life, as well as the social.

"It was a large church," he recalls, "seating over 4000 and I knew no one would know me. I sat very near the door, just in case I did not like the preacher. The service started, and did that man preach! I never heard anything like it in all my life. I was accustomed to a nice, sweet, soothing voice, poetry and book reviews, and I could sleep well under those conditions, but there was no sleep for me that morning!

"William P. Nicholson, the speaker, preached on hell and heaven and sin, and told me Christ was the one I needed. He seemed to pick me out of that huge congregation, and speak directly to me. . . ."

That Sunday morning, Percy B. Crawford accepted the Savior; and the Christian world knows his eminent usefulness since that day. Following study at the Bible Institute of Los Angeles and at Wheaton College, he has become widely known for his outstanding radio and television ministry to youth and for his service as president of King's College in New York State. And he is just one of thousands led to Christ by William P. Nicholson.

From sea fever to soul-winning—this is the summary of this Irishman's life! Saved from the raging of the sea by the mercy of God, and later to be saved from sea fever by God's salvation received one morning by the fireside in his own home; and then beside the sea, under the stars, making that full heart surrender by which he was filled with the Spirit and became a winner of souls.

Chapter Sixteen

EUGENIA PRICE
The Buoyant Life

Eugenia Price is a mid-twentieth-century miracle of God's grace.

From paganism she has come to full persuasion of Christian faith. From the broad way that leads to destruction of body and soul she has turned into the narrow way that leads to life eternal. From a selfishly ambitious career in journalism and script writing for radio and television she has made complete surrender of heart to the Savior; and from self-centeredness and smug self-satisfaction she has come into selfless service for the Crucified One.

When Genie Price was converted to Christ she was turned inside out—"a new creation in Christ Jesus"—so much so she hardly recognized herself. Before long, as told so graphically in her autobiography, *The Burden Is Light!,* she found that the nail-scarred hand of the Master was pointing her to fields of service that she would never have planned for herself. Wholeheartedly she entered deeply into fellowship with God, and into helpfulness to her fellow men. Then came a period of concern and confusion, because of darkness, bewilderment, and dismay.

Genie Price was being crowded into a corner, apparently by circumstances beyond her control, and not until she had thereby been brought to a crisis did she realize that her Lord was thus leading her to the end of herself. In her excellent statement, *He Is My Victorious Life,* she recalls:

"I had been a believer in Jesus Christ for something more than five years, when a situation arose which sent me plummeting into a kind of darkness which was new, even to one who had lived in darkness for such a long time! For once, so far as I could honestly see, I had *not* caused this trouble. I felt a victim. I hurled questions at God up through my darkness. The questions turned to rebellion and for two weeks during the month of September, 1954, I sat and stared at the floor. There were three weeks left before my fall schedule of speaking dates began, but I still had to write and direct a dramatic radio program once a week. Other than that, I sat in my close, lightless despair and suffered a depression I would not attempt to describe. . . ."

This darkness and depression came after Genie had written her autobiography, *The Burden Is Light!* Up until this time she had not fully learned that our warfare is not against flesh and blood but against spiritual forces of wickedness. Not infrequently after testimony for Christ is given, there comes a deep testing of one's faith. That was her situation. But let her tell her own story:

"My friend and associate, Ellen Riley, tried to maneuver telephone conversation with the one person whom she knew could reach me—our dear friend, Anna Mow. I avoided her. I couldn't imagine actually discussing it with anyone. Then one day I answered the telephone 'by mistake.' It was Anna. I dedicated my daily devotional book, *Share My Pleasant Stones,* to her for what she has meant to me spiritually, and her influence was climaxed by what she said to me that day. I told her I was horrified at myself. I fairly yelled into the telephone: 'How could this be the writer of *Unshackled* and *Discoveries* and *The Burden Is Light?* None of it must be true! If it is—why am I like this?'

"Anna Mow had a marvelous laugh. She laughed and it made me angry, but it stopped me long enough for her to say:

"'Of course, the things you've written are all true. You weren't witnessing to Eugenia Price, were you? When you've stood on all those platforms speaking, have you been witnessing to *you*? You certainly have not. You've been witnessing to Jesus Christ. And NOTHING CHANGES HIM!"

"I had to force her to more specifics."

"'But, Anna, I feel so pagan!'

"She laughed again.

'Well, go on and act pagan! That won't change Jesus Christ either.'

"This stopped me. Then I started again.

"'But what if I say I have stopped believing?'

"There was just a moment's silence and no laugh this time. Just a very, very quiet steady voice with a suggestion of pain:

"'Well, that wouldn't change Him either. He'd be there waiting for you to get through doubting.'

"Saying nothing more that I remember, we hung up. My darkness lifted. But it didn't leave light. It left everything *gray*. And yet in the grayness, there seemed to be movement of some kind. Another day passed and the morning mail brought a card from Anna which said simply: 'The Lord is risen!'

I stopped complaining and became a little more livable. But nothing was changed in the bad situation and nothing seemed really changed in me. I set up a prayer time each afternoon during which I battered at God with every prayer technique about which I had ever read. He just had to do something about my problem! Nothing happened at all. I ran out of 'techniques.' Then I finally told Him I was tired talking. He seemed to say 'Good.'

"And hearing no voices, I was suddenly convinced that He cared more about the whole mess than I did! So, I began to go on, in and out of one day and then another and even though nothing happened at all, I didn't complain and I stopped trying to get people to defend Jesus Christ! I stopped turning this direction and that, spitting my questions at mere human beings who already had enough troubles of their own! I hated doing it, but I kept on getting up at 6:30 A.M. for my hour with the Lord. I got nothing out of it and I told Him so. But I got up anyway and now I know that every syllable of the Word of God which we drop into our subconscious minds stays there and becomes a *usable part* of us! Even if we don't seem to 'get it' with our conscious minds.

"Then the 'crisis' time arrived and no one was more surprised than I. On September 24, 1954, at 9 A.M. My friend Ellen had been awake late the night before and asked me to let her sleep until 9. I had been reading more or less at random and with little or no understanding, here and there in the New Testament. Then I noticed my watch. It was five minutes until 9. I remembered my promise to waken her.

"'Let her have another five minutes,' I thought. And then I recall sitting there with no particular direction to my thinking. I was asking God for nothing. I was still in the grayness and still felt empty and very *un*spiritual. As our thoughts do, when we are wool-gathering, mine flew to the big heart-breaking problem in my life at that time. Then I found myself looking at the entire period of my Christian life. Suddenly aloud to the Lord, I said, 'What does it mean to have a new life? What does it *really* mean?"

"Here I make no effort to explain anything. I received no direct 'answer' as such. But for what could have been *any* length of time in my judgment, there began a 'leading' by the Holy Spirit through the Scriptures, to one surprising spot and then another, some of which I couldn't have found otherwise without my concordance. He (the Holy Spirit) *had* to begin where He began. I shall simply list the Scriptures and add what they meant to me on that morning:

"1. Acts 4:31. 'And when they had prayed, the place was shaken where they were assembled together; and they were all filled with the Holy Ghost, and they spake the word of God with boldness.' Nothing 'shook' for me. I believe I was directed to this verse so that I could see that the believers had been filled *again* with the Spirit. A marginal note said something about one baptism and many fillings. This opened my limited experiential understanding to the potential of more and more access to *more* of God. I had opened myself in obedience to the Spirit as far as I understood up to that time. This seemed suddenly to fill me with a new eagerness and expectation! The 'movement' I had felt in the grayness speeded up. I felt very excited as I seemed compelled to turn to:

"2. The 14th chapter of John. The entire chapter seemed there just for me at that moment. I had read and reread it before, but Jesus was real in a new way and I seemed aware that HE had said '*I* will come to you'! The next verse I recall was:

"3. John 15:5, 'I am the vine, ye are the branches: He that abideth in me, and I *in him,* the same bringeth forth, etc.' I stopped with 'and I in him'! Then, I didn't seem at all surprised to find myself quickly flipping the pages of the Bible to:

"4. 2 Corinthians 5:17—'Therefore if any man be in Christ, he is a new creature; old things are passed away; behold, all things are become new.' I had used this verse over and over in writing 'conversion scenes' on *Unshackled.* Here it was NEW to me. *Everything pointed to 'newness.'* I hurried to the next verse as I followed directions of the Spirit—not being aware that He was directing me at all. Just following quickly, almost tearing the pages of my Bible in my haste.

"5. Romans 6:13—'Neither yield your members as instruments of unrighteousness unto sin: but *yield yourselves unto God,* etc.' Hadn't I done this? As far as I understood, but somehow only then did I realize about the NECESSITY of yielding my

NEW self unto God! Christ Himself had come to live within me. He was changing me. But I needed to yield ALL NEW THINGS to Him. No words describe it. But I understood about the word 'new.' There was to be a continued newness or it would be old again! Then, the 'yielding' was transacted. Calmly. No dramatics. No struggle. My troubled heart was sick of trouble. MY NEED was great enough so I made a simple transaction on the grounds of the Redemption of Christ and was specific on points about which only He an I knew! And then I kept on flipping pages and there was a Psalm and a verse I would not have been able to locate at all.

"6. Psalm 73:25—'Whom have I in heaven but *thee?* and there is none upon earth that I desire beside *thee.*' In an almost matter of fact way, I said aloud: 'Oh, yes. You.' Suddenly, I *understood* simplicity.

"Then I remembered the time. It could have been noon! And I had promised Ellen I'd waken her at 9! I looked at my watch. It was exactly nine o'clock. *All this had taken place in five minutes of earth-time.* When she was awake enough to talk, I told her. It seemed in the telling as though nothing more than a 'creative quiet time' had taken place. But she began to notice (and still insists) that I have been much easier to live with since that morning.

"Personally, I simply felt *settled.* And rested. I still had all my troubles, but one glorious fact had become clear to me out of the grayness which I had fought:

"IN JESUS CHRIST HIMSELF WAS EVERYTHING I NEEDED FOR EVERYTHING IN MY LIFE!"

And what did this gracious crisis experience mean to God's servant?

As a result, there were many things new in her life. There was a new level of understanding with the Savior, a complete willingness to let Him be Himself in her life. Her testimony was more about the Savior than about His salvation. She has said: "I did not consciously feel proud. But I felt *secure* and *simplified*. I didn't need to label what had happened to me theologically. I wouldn't have known how anyway."

There was a new insight into the Word of God, and thereby into the Person of the Lord Jesus Christ. There were new fields of service, and new energy and strength for the demands made upon her.

There was a greater capacity for God in her life, as she has said. "I made room for Him ... He knew where I was in the entangling process of September 24, 1954. Only He knew *exactly* how much had been re-created in my depths."

There was newness of understanding, for Genie learned that she found the Savior in reality in the fiery furnace of affliction and testing. She found the Savior to be with her in every testing, just as truly as the three young Hebrews experienced the Presence with them in Nebuchadnezzar's furnace. As the furnace roared around her, through prayer and tears she completed her book of daily devotional readings: *Share My Pleasant Stones.*

Likewise she learned that no one is a "special case" to the Lord, and that nothing is too hard for Him. And best of all, she found that the Lord Jesus Himself is her victory, for victory is Somebody, not some thing.

That awareness and assurance did not come instantly and automatically to her, but was learned in the daily walk and talk with Him. On that September morning He had "settled" her, established her in Himself, wherefore she could say: "My experience of the next three years caused me to be 'at home' with Christ and with Christians as I had never been. He spoiled the thought of life without Him even for one hour. He used those three years and particularly did He use the new darkness and the new rebellion of this year to show me that:

1) HE MEANT IT WHEN HE SAID HE'D BE WITH ME ALWAYS;
2) I NEED TO BE MELTED INTO BEING WILLING TO BE VICTORIOUS;
3) MY NEED IS THE MOST GLORIOUS POSSESSION I HAVE OUTSIDE OF CHRIST HIMSELF;
4) HIS LOVE IS SO MUCH GREATER AND SO MUCH MORE RECREATIVE THAN WE CAN POSSIBLY CONCEIVE AND WE EXPERIENCE IT WHEN WE STOP RESISTING."

Testings have come to Eugenia Price since the crisis of the deeper life, and more of them will come in the days ahead; but the Holy Spirit will continue to show her the reality that "in all these things we are more than conquerors through Him that loved us."

Such is the buoyant life: out of bewilderment and blackness into the blessing of moment by moment fellowship with the strong Son of God!

Chapter Seventeen

CHARLES G. TRUMBULL
The Victorious Life

*T*wo of Bunyan's leading characters in *Pilgrim's Progress,* Mr. Valiant-for-Truth and Mrs. Standfast, are seventeenth-century portraits of twentieth-century Charles G. Trumbull. As editor of the *Sunday School Times* he was a prominent leader among evangelicals, energetic and effective in his stand for the faith "once delivered to the saints," friendly, approachable, courteous, always considerate and fair with those with whom he had to disagree because of the truth.

Most of all, Mr. Trumbull was a living example of the *life that wins;* the life that knows the reality of Galatians 2:20: "I am crucified with Christ: nevertheless I live; yet not I, but Christ liveth in me; and the life which I now live in the flesh I live by the faith of the Son of God, who loved me, and gave himself for me."

So dynamic and satisfying was the transformation that came to Dr. Trumbull by the indwelling Savior that everywhere, by life, word, and pen, he gave testimony to *the life that is Christ.* He was a key factor in the formation of the Victorious Life Testimony which sponsors the American Keswick in New Jersey.

We who knew Dr. Trumbull in his later years remember a buoyant, joyous, earnest, unassuming, Spirit-filled Christian journalist and leader. The life that abides in Christ and draws all of its resources from the risen Savior was to him a wonderful reality. It was certainly not some fancy or fanaticism to him.

Fortunately, Dr. Trumbull's testimony has been retained for us in the very excellent little pamphlet: *The Life That Wins.*

Originally this testimony was given before the National Convention of the Presbyterian Brotherhood of America at its meeting in St. Louis in 1911.

"There is only one life that wins; and that is the life of Jesus Christ. Every man may have that life; every man may live that life.

"I do not mean that every man may be Christlike; I mean something very much better than that. I do not mean that a man may always have Christ's help; I mean something better than that. I do not mean that a man may have power from Christ; I mean something very much better than power. And I do not mean that a man shall be merely saved from his sins and kept from sinning; I mean something better than even that victory."

The pattern of Dr. Trumbull's experience is like that of every other man of God who has come to know that "Christ liveth in me, and the life which I now live in the flesh, I live by the faith of the Son of God." That pattern is first failure, then a sense of need. Thereafter comes an awareness of the secret of the indwelling Savior, a secret so simplE that most Christians stumble over it or are unaware of it.

Then follows a definite meeting with the Lord Jesus and surrender of heart and will that brings one into personal realization of *the life that is Christ*. Thereafter there is the outflow of that life, likened by Dr. Trumbull and many others to the "rivers of living water" spoken of by the Lord Jesus in John 7:38.

Candidly did Dr. Trumbull tell of the conscious needs that existed in his life. First, he was aware of great fluctuations in his spiritual life: On occasion in conscious fellowship with the Savior, and then again down in the depths of defeat. There were seasons of lifting up because of a searching message or a Spirit-filled book; but thereafter came the decline. He observed: "Sometimes by a single failure before temptation, sometimes by a gradual downhill process, my best experiences would be lost, and I would find myself back on the lower levels. . . . It seemed to me that it ought to be possible for me to live habitually on a high plane of close fellowship with God, as I saw certain other men doing, and as I was not doing."

Then there was the matter of "failure before besetting sins." He did believe that in certain areas he could be more than conqueror, but not in others. Despite earnest prayer for deliverance, abiding victory was not his experience.

The third conscious lack was "in the matter of dynamic, convincing spiritual power that would work miracle changes in other men's lives." He was an active Christian, engaged in many duties and responsibilities. He had to say: "I was even doing personal work—the hardest kind of all; talking with people, one by one, about giving themselves to my Savior! *But I wasn't seeing results.*"

This lack of effectiveness he rationalized with the old assurance (so much used by the enemy of souls) that it wasn't for him to see results; that he could safely leave that to the Lord if he did his part. Such rationalization over spiritual barrenness left him heartsick, however.

Dr. Trumbull knew that he had received the Lord Jesus as his personal Savior. Certainly he was most sound in the faith, and active in Christian service. He sought to satisfy the hunger of his heart and to excuse his ineffectiveness by his orthodoxy regarding the Person and work of the Savior.

The hunger of heart became more intense when he heard a preacher speak on Ephesians 4:12, 13; especially on those words "Till we all come . . . unto a perfect man, unto the measure of the stature of the fullness of Christ." Dr. Trumbull testified:

"As I followed it I was amazed, bewildered. I could not follow him. He was beyond my depth. He was talking about Christ, unfolding Christ, in a way that I admitted was utterly unknown to me."

That hunger was sharpened by his observation of another servant of the Lord who enjoyed habitual consciousness of the presence of the Savior with him always. The climax of need came at the World Missionary Conference in Edinburgh (1910) when he went eagerly to hear a message on "The Resources of the Christian Life." Said Dr. Trumbull:

"I expected him to give us a series of definite things that we could do to strengthen our Christian life; and I knew I needed them. But his opening words showed me my mistake, while they made my heart leap with a new joy. What he said was something like this: '*The resources of the Christian life, my friends, are just—Jesus Christ.*'"

That was all. But that was enough.

The crisis of the deeper life came to God's needy and trusting servant that summer. He was attending a young people's missionary conference; and, in his own words, "was faced by a week of daily work there for which I knew I was miserably, hopelessly unfit and incompetent." In the providence of God the first message by a fellow speaker was on "The Water of Life," from John 7:37–39. He heard again that the "rivers of living water" in a Christian's life should flow continuously and irresistibly, not intermittently. Again let Editor Trumbull speak for himself:

"The next morning, Sunday, alone in my room, I prayed it out with God, as I asked Him to show me the way out. If there was a conception of Christ that I did not have, and that I needed, because it was the secret of some of these other lives I had seen or heard of, a conception better than any I had yet had, and beyond me, I asked God to give it to me. I had with me the sermon I had heard, 'To me to live is Christ,' and I rose from my knees and studied it. Then I prayed again. And God, in His longsuffering patience, forgiveness, and love, gave me what I asked for. He gave me a new Christ—wholly new in the conception and consciousness of Christ that now became mine.

"Wherein was the change? It is hard to put it into words, and yet it is, oh, so new, and real, and wonderful, and miracle-working in both my own life and the lives of others.

"To begin with, I realized for the first time that the many references throughout the New Testament to Christ in you, and you in Christ, Christ our life, and abiding in Christ, are literal, actual, blessed fact, and not figures of speech. How the 15th chapter of John thrilled with the new life as I read it now! And the 3rd of Ephesians, 14 to 21. And Galatians 2:20. And Philippians 1:21."

No longer was Dr. Trumbull's faith only in the Christ who had died on the cross for our sins. His faith was now also in the Savior who dwells within the believer. "At last I realized," he declared, "that Jesus Christ was actually and literally within me; and even more than that: that He had constituted Himself my very life, taking me into union with Himself—my body, mind, and spirit—while I still had my own identity and free will and full moral responsibility. . . . It meant that I need never again ask Him to help me as though He were one and I another; but rather simply to do His work, His will, in me, and with me, and through me. . . . Jesus Christ had constituted Himself my life—not as a figure of speech, remember, but as a literal, actual fact. . . ."

From deep and vital experience with the risen Savior and because of the constant drawing on His life, the believer in Christ realizes experientially *the life that wins*. Dr. Trumbull learned that the flow of that life was dependent on two simple conditions. After having received the Lord Jesus as personal Savior there is *first*, surrender, an absolute and unconditional surrender to the Savior as Lord and Master of one's life, irrespective of the cost; and *second*, the quiet act of faith, apart from any feeling or immediate evidence that God does set the trusting soul wholly free from the law of sin.

And how does this fullness of life, *the life that is Christ,* demonstrate itself in the experience of the believer? Let Dr. Trumbull speak for himself:

"The three great lacks or needs of which I spoke at the opening have been miraculously met.

"1. There has been a fellowship with God utterly differing from and infinitely better than anything I had ever known in all my life before.

"2. There has been an utterly new kind of victory, victory-by-freedom, over certain besetting sins—the old ones that used to throttle and wreck me—when I have trusted Christ for this freedom.

"3. And, lastly, the spiritual results in service have given me such a sharing of the joy of heaven as I never knew was possible on earth. Six of my most intimate friends, most of them mature Christians, soon had their lives completely revolutionized by Christ, laying hold on Him in this new way and receiving Him unto all the fullness of God. . . . A white-haired man of seventy found a peace in life and a joy in prayer that he had long ago given up as impossible for him. Life fairly teems with the miracle-evidences of what Christ is willing and able to do for other lives through anyone who just turns over the keys to His complete indwelling.

"Jesus Christ does not want to be our helper; He wants to be our life. He does not want us to work for Him. He wants us to let Him do His work through us, using us as we use a pencil to write with—better still, using us as one of the fingers on His hand."

Such indeed is *the life that wins;* and Dr. Trumbull was able *by that life* to lead many others into the life of victory. Very properly did the Victorious Life Testimony select as its scriptural motto, Philippians 1:21—"To me to live is Christ."

Chapter Eighteen

WALTER L. WILSON

The Yielded Life

With regard to my own experience with the Holy Spirit, I may say that the transformation in my own life on January 14, 1914, was greater, much greater than the change which took place when I was saved December 21, 1896."

Thus writes Dr. Walter L. Wilson, the "beloved physician" of Kansas City, an excellent teacher of God's Word and preacher of the Gospel, President Emeritus of Kansas City Bible College, Pastor of Central Bible Church of that city, and known throughout the world because of his writings and Bible conference ministry. Beyond these accomplishments, which include, of course, his effective ministry of healing as a physician, he is pre-eminently a winner of souls.

And what might be Dr. Wilson's secret, if any?

God's servant tells us that after he was converted that December night in 1896, he became a lover of the Scriptures, and became diligent in teaching, preaching and distributing tracts. Much effort, however, seemed to produce little result, and no apparent success followed his labors. This ineffectiveness troubled him, but he was told by others "not to look for results, but only to be busy at seed sowing."

Then God gave to him a great challenge, as is so often the case for the Lord's people. Just as a white-haired old man in Brooklyn admonished the energetic Moody to honor the Holy Spirit, and an elderly friend wrote a steamer letter to the young missionary, John Hyde, to seek the fullness of the Spirit; just so a man of God was used by the Almighty to stir the heart of Walter Wilson. In 1913 a servant of the Lord from France was visiting in the Wilson home, and inquired, "What is the Holy Spirit to you?"

Dr. Wilson's answer was orthodox: "He is one of the Persons of the God-Head ... a Teacher, a Guide; the third Person of the Trinity."

The missionary corrected Dr. Wilson by pointing out that he had given to the Holy Spirit a place of insignificance and inferiority. "He is just as great," said the missionary, "just as precious, just as needful as the other two Persons of the Trinity. But still you have not answered my question, what is He to you?"

To this Dr. Wilson had to reply truthfully, "He is nothing to me. I have no contact with Him, no personal relationship, and could get along quite well without Him."

The doctor was surprised and grieved by the answer he had given so truthfully; and his friend's reply filled him with fear because he said, "It is because of this that your life is so fruitless even though your efforts are so great. If you will seek personally to know the Holy Spirit, He will transform your life."

The beloved physician was fearful of following such advice because he had been taught that the believer can have nothing personally to do with the Holy Spirit lest he become a fanatic. He was fearful, too, of giving an inferior place to the Savior by exalting the Spirit above the Son of God. These doubts and questions he made known to a fellow Christian teacher who explained to him from the Scriptures that only by the Holy Spirit could Christ be made known to him and through him to others.

Then came January 14, 1914. Dr. James M. Gray, at that time a clergyman of the Reformed Episcopal Church, and later the beloved and revered president of Moody Bible Institute, was speaking in Kansas City on Romans 12:1. Dr. Wilson recalls the impact of that message:

"Leaning over the pulpit, he said, 'Have you noticed that this verse does not tell us to whom we should give our bodies? It is not the Lord Jesus Who asks for it. He has His own body. It is not the Father Who asks for it. He remains upon His throne. Another has come to earth without a body. God could have made a body for Him as He did for Jesus, but He did not do so. God gives you the privilege and the indescribable honour of presenting your bodies to the Holy Spirit, to be His dwelling place on earth. If you have been washed in the Blood of the Lamb then yours is a holy body, washed whiter than snow, and will be accepted by the Spirit when you give it. Will you do so now?'"

At the conclusion of the service, Dr. Wilson and his father-in-law, who had attended the meeting with him, returned home. Each went at once to his own room. Utterly heartbroken over his fruitless life, yet filled with a great hope because of the message he had heard from a teacher in whom he had all confidence, Dr. Wilson lay upon the carpet of his study, prostrate in God's presence. Hear his testimony:

"There, in the quiet of that late hour, I said to the Holy Spirit, 'My Lord, I have mistreated You all my Christian life. I have treated You like a servant. When I wanted You I called for You; when I was about to engage in some work I beckoned You to come and help me perform my task. I have kept You in the place of a servant. I have sought to use You only as a willing servant to help me in my self-appointed and chosen work. I shall do so no more. Just now I give You this body of mine; from my head to my feet, I give it to You. I give You my hands, my limbs, my eyes and lips, my brain; all that I am within and without, I hand over to You for You to live in it the life that You please. You may send this body to Africa, or lay it on a bed with cancer. You may blind the eyes, or send me with Your message to Tibet. You may take this body to the Eskimos, or send it to a hospital with pneumonia. It is your body from this moment on. Help yourself to it. Thank You, my Lord, I believe You have accepted it, for in Romans twelve and one You said "acceptable unto God." Thank You again, my Lord, for taking me. We now belong to each other.'"

And what were the results of that surrender of body and appropriation of the fullness of the Holy Spirit?

The very next morning two young ladies came to the office to sell advertising, as they had done previously. Up to that time the doctor had never spoken to them about the Lord Jesus because his lips had been his own and he had used them for business purposes. Now that his lips had been given away, the Holy Spirit was to use them; and He did so at once. Out of brief conversation and testimony to his visitors, Dr. Wilson led both of them to a saving knowledge of Jesus Christ. They were the first fruits of a great harvest of souls that Dr. Wilson won for the Savior.

Hundreds of thousands have been thrilled and challenged by the doctor's experiences in soul winning, such as he had recounted in *The Romance of a Doctor's Visits*. For example, in the account of "The Little Man in a Big City" he tells of his being alone in the great city of New York. Before he went out for a business appointment he had prayer in his hotel room, and requested: "My Lord, this is a large city of seven million people, and I am just a weak, unknown servant of Thine with no knowledge of the city and no acquaintance with the hungry hearts that may be there. Thou alone dost know whom Thou hast been dealing with. Here is my body—my feet and my lips. Wilt Thou take them today to some troubled heart and speak through me thy Words of light and life? Thank You, Lord, I believe You will do it."

As he walked eastward on Thirty-second Street he passed a stationery shop and noticed a small leather-covered notebook in the window. This brought to mind his need of a book in which to keep his prayer list. Upon entering the shop he inquired of the little German owner about the notebook. The size and the price were satisfactory; and the shopkeeper began to wrap it up. Just then Dr. Wilson said, "Do you know what I expect to do with this little book?"

The storekeeper did not know, and was astonished to learn that it was to be used as a prayer book. Thereupon he began to unwrap the package saying, "I am sorry, my friend, but this is a blank book; it is not a prayer book."

That was just the opening Dr. Wilson needed. He explained that he made his own prayer book, using the left-hand pages for petitions and the right-hand ones for the answers. Then he added his testimony of knowing the Lord Jesus as His Savior, and invited the shopkeeper to do the same.

The reply was not surprising. "Mister, I have tried to find Gott for many years. I have gone about Manhattan and Brooklyn and the Bronx, night after night, attending many services, but failed always to find Gott. Can you tell me how to get to Him?"

After explanation of the Scripture that the Lord Jesus is the Way, the Truth, and the Life, Dr. Wilson led his new friend to the Savior. The quest of the years had come to an end, for now the shopkeeper knew the Lord Jesus for himself.

And for the soul winner only twenty minutes had elapsed from the prayer in the hotel room to the winning of another soul to Christ, because the life and lips of the servant belonged to the Holy Spirit.

The quiet impact of the spirit of God through Walter L. Wilson, both in his teaching and his writing, has been felt the world over. For example, a missionary had served many years in Tibet with such little effectiveness that he determined to return to the homeland. As a result he finally packed his belongings, said farewell to his new friends in that far-off roof of the world, and prepared to leave for the United States. This is his story:

"A short time before I was to leave the country I took a journey across the hills to the post office to leave a forwarding address and to obtain what mail might be there. In the mail which I received was a copy of 'The Evangelical Christian.' I opened the magazine in the post office and was struck by the title 'Whose Body Is Yours?' by Dr. Walter L. Wilson. . . . I read the article through carefully and then read it through again. I went back home slowly, thoughtfully and deeply stirred in my spirit. There, kneeling among my goods, I gave my body to the Spirit and received Him as the Lord of my life. At once my spirit was relieved. Hope sprang anew in my heart. The work of my Lord looked quite different. I had found the power for service. I unpacked my things and told the Lord that since my body was His, I could now expect that He would use it. The results were wonderful. The transformation was indescribable. God began to make my ministry fruitful and I can testify to you that this is really God's path of blessing."

Dr. Wilson's testimony in *The Evangelical Christian* brought many letters to the editor among which was this one:

"In one of the issues of your magazine there was printed an article entitled 'Whose Body Is Yours?' It was written by a man who explained how one day he came to the place where he made an absolute surrender to Christ—his hands, his feet, his whole body, his plans, his future, everything he placed at Jesus' feet. At the time I read this article I was in great difficulty spiritually and had not a single soul to guide me out here, not a soul it seemed, who had either the desire or time to talk about spiritual things with me. And then I picked up your magazine and read this article. For a whole day I walked up and down my room hardly able to contain myself from shouting—the relief was almost more than I could bear—the problem had been solved for me, and I just then and there did exactly what that man did, repeating to Christ his very words and making the same bargain. What this article meant to my soul eternity will show. The fruit of that man's life is surely very, very precious fruit. Since that day I have never looked back, but am pressing onward, and after these days of chastening, which I am going through, are over, I trust I shall likewise be as fruitful as he."

The doctor's secret of soul winning is the simplicity of taking God at His Word. In his case it was obeying implicitly the exhortation of Romans 12:1—"that ye present your bodies a living sacrifice, holy, acceptable unto God, which is your reasonable service"—and in so doing finding that his body in reality belonged to the Holy Spirit who could use it when and where He would. Since that January night Dr. Wilson has proved in a multitude of ways the authority and power, the wisdom and knowledge of the Holy Spirit as the leader of one's life, and as the Lord of the harvest. Well do we take heed to Dr. Wilson's exhortation: "I intreat each of you to go directly to the Holy Spirit Himself, to give Him your body, and then look to Him constantly to do what He wants with that body for the glory and honor of our Lord Jesus Christ."

Chapter Nineteen

JOHN ALLAN WOOD
The Holy Life

Nineteenth-century J. A. Wood of North Attleboro, Massachusetts, was as ardent a Wesleyan as eighteenth-century Jonathan Edwards of Northampton was a convinced Calvinist; and yet their experience of the immediacy and power of God in their lives was almost identical.

The teaching and testimony of Pastor Wood has been retained for us in his writings, principally the volume entitled *Purity and Maturity,* and also, *Perfect Love.* Converted at the age of ten, he was a devout lad with desire to know the things of God, and with delight in prayer and obedience to the Almighty.

During the first five or six years of his Christian life he was often perplexed and distressed with doubts as to the reality of his conversion, because it did not seem to him as dramatic and deeply emotional as was true of some. He would later say, however: "After many and severe trials on this point, the Lord enabled me to settle the matter; and thousand thanks to His blessed name, many years have passed since I have doubted for a moment the verify of my early conversion."

While preparing for the ministry he found that he himself, his old Adamic nature, was his greatest hindrance to growth in Christian experience. Of those years he wrote:

"During this period I was often convicted of remaining corruption of heart and of my need of purity. I desired to be a decided Christian and a useful member of the church; but was often conscious of deep-rooted inward evils and tendencies in my heart unfriendly to godliness. My bosom-foes troubled me more than all my foes from without. They struggled for the ascendancy. They marred my peace. They obscured my spiritual vision. They were the instruments of severe temptation. They interrupted my communion with God. They crippled my efforts to do good. They invariably sided with Satan. They occupied a place in my heart which I knew should be possessed by the Holy Spirit. They were the greatest obstacles to my growth in grace, and rendered my service to God but partial.

"I was often more strongly convicted of my need of inward purity than I ever had been of my need of pardon. God showed me the importance and the necessity of holiness as clear as a sunbeam. I seldom studied the Bible without conviction of my fault in not coming up to the Scripture standard of salvation."

Although convinced of his need of complete dedication to the Savior and the fullness of the Spirit in his life, he held "no clear or definite ideas in regard to the blessing of perfect love, but thought of it, and taught it, as only a deeper work of grace, or a little more religion." He declared: "I became somewhat prejudiced against the Bible terms *'sanctification,' 'holiness,'* and *'perfection,'* and disliked very much to hear persons use them in speaking of their experience; and opposed the profession of holiness as a blessing distinct from regeneration. I became prejudiced against the special advocates of holiness; and at camp meetings and in other places discouraged and opposed direct efforts for its promotion."

Wood was ordained to the gospel ministry, and became a devoted pastor and an acceptable preacher. Hungry of heart for purity and power in his life, however, he came into contact with some "whose experience in piety possessed a *richness, depth,* and *power*" which he did not have and consequently he says he "was preaching to some who enjoyed more religion than their pastor."

To continue his testimony:

"Through the entire summer of 1858 I was seeking holiness, but kept the matter to myself. During this time none of the professors of holiness said anything to me on the subject, but, as I have learned since, were praying for me night and day. God only knew the severe struggles I had that long summer, during many hours of which I lay on my face in my study, begging Jesus to cleanse my poor, unsanctified heart; and yet was unwilling to make a public avowal of my feelings, or to ask the prayers of God's people for my sanctification.

"The Binghamton district camp-meeting commenced that year the 1st day of September, and about eighty of the members of my charge attended it with me. . . .

"On the last day of the meeting, a few minutes before preaching, a faithful member of the church came to me weeping, and said, 'Brother Wood, there is no use in trying to dodge this question. You know your duty. If you will lead the way, and define your position as a seeker of entire sanctification, you will find that many of the members of your charge have a mind to do the same.' The Lord had so humbled my heart that I was willing to do anything to obtain relief. After a few moments' reflection I replied, 'Immediately after preaching I will appoint a meeting in our tent on the subject of holiness, and will ask the prayers of the church for my own soul.'

"Glory be to God! The Rubicon was passed. The moment of decision was the moment of triumph. In an instant I felt a giving away in my heart so sensible and powerful that it appeared physical rather than spiritual; a moment after I felt an indescribable sweetness permeating my entire being. It was a sweetness as real and as sensible to my soul as ever the sweetest honey to my taste. I immediately walked up into the stand.

Just as the preacher gave out his text,—Eccl. 12:13, 'Let us hear the conclusion of the whole matter,' etc.,—the baptism of fire and power came upon me.

"For me to describe what I then realized is utterly impossible. It was such as I need not attempt to describe to those who have felt and tasted it, and such as I can not describe to the comprehension of those whose hearts have never realized it. I was conscious that Jesus had me in his arms, and that the Heaven of heavens was streaming through and through my soul in such beams of light and overwhelming love and glory, as can never be uttered. *The half can never be told!*

"It was like marching through the gates of the city to the bosom of Jesus, and taking a full draught from the river of life."

The man of God then knew for himself the melting, the cleansing, and the filling of the Holy spirit with His sin-consuming power. Like so many others, it was Pastor Wood's experience that the blessing of God did not come into his life until the last barrier or hindrance was broken down. After thus coming to know the immediacy of God in his life he could say:

"A willingness to humble myself, and take a decided stand for holiness, and face opposition to it in the church, and take the odium of being an advocate of holiness in Binghamton, where the doctrine had been trailing in the dust for years, constituted the turning-point with me. After I reached that point of complete submission, I had no consciousness of making any special effort in believing; my whole being seemed simply, and without effort, to be borne away to Jesus."

The deep dealing of God with His servant was not confined to that single experience; rather, he could say: "From that hour the deep and solid communion with God, and the rich baptisms of love and power have been 'unspeakable and full of glory' ... at times I have had an overwhelming sense of the

Divine presence, and a sacred unction has pervaded my whole being. Especially this has been my experience while called to defend this glorious salvation. . . . There was a divine fragrance and sweetness imparted to my soul when the Savior cleansed and filled it with pure love, that has ever remained with me, and I trust it ever will. . . . To know that God is mine; to feel that He dwells in my heart, rules my will, my affections, my desires; to know that He loves me ten thousand times better than I love him—oh, what solid bliss is this!"

And what were the lasting effects of this crisis experience in the life of God's servant? Let him speak for himself:

"Some of the precious results of the cleansing power of Jesus in my soul have been:—

"1. A sacred nearness to God my Savior. The distance between God and my soul has appeared annihilated, and the glory and presence of divinity have often appeared like a flood of sunlight, surrounding, penetrating, and pervading my whole being. . . .

"2. A sense of indescribable sweetness in Christ. The fact that he is 'the rose of Sharon'; 'the lily of the valley'; 'the brightness of his [the Father's] glory', and 'altogether lovely', has at times so penetrated my soul as to thrill and fill it with ecstatic rapture. How lovely has the dear Savior appeared to my soul, and how strong the attraction my heart has felt toward him! How I love him!

"3. A deep, realizing sense of spiritual things. Bible truth has appeared transformed into solid realities. The doctrines of the gospel have become to me tangible facts, and my soul has triumphed in them as eternal *verities*.

"4. A surprising richness and fullness of meaning in the Scriptures, which I had not before realized. Many portions of the Word, which I had hitherto but little understood, now appeared full of meaning, and exceedingly precious. . . .

"5. A triumph over temptation more complete and habitual. When Satan comes he finds the sympathies and affinities of my soul strongly against him; hence he receives no favorable response. . . .

"6. A great increase in spiritual power. This I have realized in my closest devotions, in my pastoral duties, and especially in the ministrations of the blessed truth. Blessed by the Lord, I have learned by experience that men may receive the Holy Ghost in *measure* limited only by their *capacity to receive,* and feeble *ability* to *endure.* . . .

"This increase of power has delivered me from slavish fear of man, or of future evil. It has given me such love to the Savior and to his glorious gospel as to make all my duties sweet and delightful. . . .

"7. A clear and distinct witness of purity through the blood of Jesus. . . .

"8. A disposition to tell the blessed story of Christ, and his 'great salvation.' O for a thousand seraph tongues to publish the glad tidings to perishing men!

"In this narrative of my religious experience I have endeavored to give a simple statement of facts, regardless of what mistaken good men or wicked men may think or say. I would as soon deny God as to flee before the offense of the cross, or quail under the reproach of Christ. Like Peter and John, I 'can not but speak the things which I have seen and heard.'"

To God's servant the crisis of the deeper life resulted in perfect love that continued to flood his soul.

The questions that occur to us as we read his testimony were asked of Pastor wood in his day. "Perfect love" he defined as *"pure love filling the heart.* That is all! . . . Our perfection is *in Christ,* as the perfection of the branch is in the vine. Grace is derived from Christ only by a union with him, as the branch to the vine. . . ."

Some inquired: "Does Christian perfection exclude growth in grace?" To this he replied, "By no means. The pure in heart grow *faster* than any others. . . . There is no standing still in a *religious life* nor in a *sinful life.* We must either *progress* or *regress.* . . . Again, our capacities and powers are improvable and expansive, and we must proportionately grow in holiness. . . ."

The further question was then asked: "How can holiness be perfect and yet progressive?" His answer was: "Perfection in *quality* does not exclude increase in *quantity.* Beyond entire sanctification there is no increase in *purity,* as that which is pure cannot be more pure; but there may be unlimited increase in *expansion* and *quantity.*"

Christian holiness as understood by Pastor Wood does not exclude the possibility of temptation and a liability to sin. "Holiness secures the safest possible conditions on earth. . . . Grace never induces presumption."

Nor does Christian perfection produce perfect knowledge and infallibility of judgment. Certainly the apostle Peter was filled with the Spirit of God, and it is equally certain that he made errors in judgment. The fullness of the Spirit does not of necessity deliver from the infirmities of human nature, such as "slowness of understanding, errors of judgment, mistakes in practice, erratic imaginations, a treacherous memory, etc."

One more question: "What is the grand secret of holy living?" To this God's servant replied: "It is to *obtain* and *retain* the *perpetual presence, fullness* and *illumination* of the Holy Ghost. 'He shall abide with you for ever.'

"1. He will *subdue* your lusts and propensities. 'Walk in the Spirit, and ye shall not fulfill the lusts of the flesh.'

"2. He will impart *liberty.* 'Where the Spirit of the Lord is, there is liberty.'

"3. He *reveals* the things of Christ. 'He shall receive of mine and show it unto you.' 'He shall testify of me.'

"4. He presents the *truth* of God and the things of God to the mind. 'The sword of the Spirit is the Word of God.' 'Even so the things of God knoweth no man, but the Spirit of God.' 'But God hath revealed them unto us by his Spirit.'

"5. He imparts *light* and *wisdom.* 'He will guide you into all truth.'

"6. He *sustains* in the hour of *affliction.* 'I will not leave you comfortless.' 'I will send the comforter.'

"7. He imparts the *virtues* of a *holy character.* 'The fruit of the Spirit is love, joy, peace, long-suffering, gentleness, goodness, faith, meekness, temperance.

"8. He gives the *witness* of adoption and salvation. 'The Spirit beareth witness with our spirit, that we are the children of God.'

"9. He imparts the divine *image*—the *heavenly signet*—to the soul. 'Ye are sealed with the Holy Spirit of promise.'

"10. He is the *source* and *author* of all love to God. 'The love of God is shed abroad in our hearts by the Holy Ghost which is given unto us.'

"11. He is the source of *strength* and *success.* 'Not by might, nor by power, but by my Spirit, saith the Lord of hosts.'

"12. His presence and work make the soul a temple, sacred to the service of God. 'Know ye not that ye are the temple of God, and that the Spirit of God dwelleth in you? If any man defile the temple of God, him shall God destroy; for the temple of God is holy, which temple ye are.'

"Not by might nor by power [i.e., by human energy and effort], but by my Spirit" was the secret of this exchanged life. What once had been painful trying had become perfect trusting. Weakness had been turned into strength, sighing into song, and total failure into triumph—all because he learned to be filled with the Holy Spirit, and to walk in the Spirit.

Chapter Twenty

W. IAN THOMAS
The Adventurous Life

*S*ome Christians learn that the Lord can make life an adventure. Major W. Ian Thomas of England is one of them.

The Major is every inch a soldier. With his infantry battalion he served in the British Expeditionary Forces in Belgium at the outset of World War II, and took part in the evacuation at Dunkirk. Often in combat, in France, Italy, Greece, and elsewhere during that long war, he found the Lord Jesus to be his complete sufficiency. The Major is likewise a soldier of the Cross, faithful to the Captain of our salvation. He has found life an adventure with God and for Him, a pageant of triumph in Christ.

Reared in a "respectable" middle-class English home, he was taken to church and taught its precepts. He learned little or nothing of the Bible, however, either at home or in the church attended by the family. At the age of twelve he was invited to a Bible study group of the Crusaders' Union by a lad of thirteen who, during that year, had received Christ as his Savior. The Bible began to be meaningful to young Ian, and the following summer at the age of thirteen he was converted to Christ at a Crusaders' Union Camp. That decision was made when he was alone, and simply by praying earnestly, "Lord Jesus, please be my Savior!"

At the age of fifteen he felt convinced that he should devote all of his life to the service of the Lord Jesus. He told God that he would become a missionary. He began to preach, out in the open air at Hampstead Heath, at that early age. He was also actively engaged in Sunday school work, as well as in the Crusaders' Bible class. Life began to be a round of ceaseless activity.

In 1956 Major Thomas came to Wheaton College in Wheaton, Illinois for a week of meetings. In sharing with the students his experience of what Jesus Christ meant to Him, he gave the following account of those early years of ceaseless but ineffective activity.

Speaking of his youthful decision to become a missionary, he said: "I began to consider the best area in which I could become a missionary, and the best means I could employ to be most effective—perfectly sincere and genuine questions." The first missionary influence on young Ian's life came through a doctor serving in Nigeria, in the Housa Band. "First impressions are often the strongest," related Major Thomas, and so it became his ambition to one day go and join the Housa Band in Nigeria, West Africa. He thought the best thing for him to do was to become a doctor. "My parents were wonderfully good," he said, "and they gave me choice of any career that I would like, and so I went, at the age of seventeen, to London University to study at St. Bartholomew's Hospital."

At the university Ian became a leader in the Inter-Varsity Fellowship group. If ever there was any evangelistic activity going on, this youthful zealot was "buzzing around the place, every holiday, every spare moment!" He started a slum club down in the East End of London. "Out of a sheer desire to win souls," he said, "to go out and get them, I was a windmill of activity, until, at the age of nineteen, every moment of my day was packed tight with doing things: preaching, talking, counseling."

In the Major's own words we continue his story. "The only thing that alarmed me was that nobody was converted! That gets a little discouraging after a bit, doesn't it? The *more* I did, the *less* happened; and it was not a question of insincerity. The prospects and environment were good; there was plenty of ammunition and plenty of target, but just *nothing* happened! I became deeply depressed, because I really loved the Lord Jesus Christ with all my heart; I wanted to be made a blessing to my fellow men. But I discovered that forever doubling and redoubling my efforts in order to win souls, rushing here and dashing there, taking part in this campaign, taking part in that campaign, preaching in the morning, preaching in the evening, talking to the Bible class, witnessing to this one, counseling with another, did nothing, nothing, nothing to change the utter barrenness, the emptiness, the uselessness of my activity. I tried to make up with noise what I lacked in effectiveness and power.

"Thus by the age of nineteen, I had been reduced to a state of complete exhaustion spiritually, until I felt that there was no point in going on; and there was certainly no point in going to Africa as a missionary, because if it was a question of energy and earnestness and zeal and *doing* things, well then, that had failed, and I did not know any other answer. I was prepared to go to Africa and be as useless there as I was already in England. There is nothing magic about getting on a boat! There is nothing magic about changing your geographical position, or putting on a little pair of tropical shorts and a sun helmet! That will not make you a soul-winner over night. Do not imagine that you will be any more spiritually effective on the mission field than you are in your own home town. Indeed, you will find it a thousand times more difficult!

"Then, one night in November, that year, just at midnight, in my room at home, I got down on my knees before God, and I just wept in sheer despair. I said, 'Oh, God, I know that I am saved. I love Jesus Christ. I am perfectly convinced that I am converted. With all my heart I have wanted to serve Thee. I have tried to my uttermost and I am a hopeless failure! So far as doing anything more, I am finished. I am not going to be a missionary. It is useless for me to continue like this. I hate this double life!' That night things happened.

"I can honestly say that I had never once heard from the lips of men the message that came to me then. I never had read it in print; but God, that night, simply focused upon me the Bible message of *Christ Who is our Life.* This was the moment He had been waiting for; seven weary years He had watched me running round and round in the wilderness! He had been waiting for the time when at last I would fall down in hopeless despair. I heard His voice: 'To me to live *is Christ.*...I am the way, the truth, *and the life....* If, when we were enemies, we were reconciled to God by the death of His Son, much more being reconciled, we shall be saved *by His life....* When *Christ who is our life* shall appear, then shall we appear with Him in glory.' Life! New Life! To me to live is *Christ!*

"It just came from every area of God's Word, and very kindly and very lovingly the Lord seemed to make it plain to me that night, through my tears of bitterness: 'You see, for seven years, with utmost sincerity, you have been trying to live *for* Me, on My behalf, the life that I have been waiting for seven years to live *through* you. I have been there the whole time. All the things you have been pleading for, all the things for which you have been asking, have been yours since the day seven years ago, at your request and invitation, I came into your heart at that Crusader boys' camp; but you see, although you have given mental consent to the truth that I have been in your heart, and have accepted it as a theory, you have lived totally ignoring *the fact.* You have been busy trying to do *for* Me all that only I can do *through* you. Now supposing I am your life, and you begin to accept it as a fact, then I am your strength!

You have been pleading and begging for that for seven years. I *am* your victory in every area of your life, if you want it! I am the One to whom it is perfectly natural to go out and win souls; and I know precisely where to go to find them. Why don't you begin to reckon upon Me and say 'Thank you.'"

That night, all in the space of an hour, Ian Thomas discovered the secret of the adventurous life.

He said: "With nothing to support the theory and without the testimony of any other known Christian to the facts, I simply said to the Lord Jesus Christ that night, 'Well, it is that or nothing! If this is true, then I am going to thank Thee for it in sheer cold-blooded faith, with no evidence to support it, and nothing but a history of failure behind me! I am going to thank Thee that if Thou art my life, and this is true, then Thou art my victory, Thou art my strength, Thou art my power, Thou art my future! Thou art the One Who is going to go out now, clothed with me to do all that I so hopelessly have been trying to do in the past seven years!' Then I went to sleep!

"I got up the next morning to an entirely different Christian life, but I want to emphasize this: I had not received one iota more than I had already had for seven years! I had had the Lord Jesus, equal to all my need and in whom I had been blessed with every spiritual blessing in heavenly things, for the whole of those seven years; but I stepped out on my way to the university that morning with a new song in my heart. I was saying, 'Lord Jesus I thank Thee for the first time in my life, this is Thy day! I no longer have the burden of running my own life. At last I have a governor capable of governing!'

"I can remember that on my way down to the university, I thought over the meeting that I was to take on the following Sunday. It was a boys' class, and I said, 'Well now Lord, thou art going to speak to that boys' class isn't it wonderful? Yesterday I thought I was going to, but *Thou* art going to now!

I thank Thee, dear Lord, for the boys that thou art going to save.' I did not know how many boys there were in that Bible class, but I began to dream dreams, and I thought, 'Well, maybe thirty will be converted.' Not bad for a start! 'For the first time in my life, I'll dare to invite boys, at the end of that meeting, to come and see me if they want to accept Jesus Christ as their Savior.' Now I had never done that in my life, and for a very good reason—I had not expected them to come, and I did not want to look a fool! Now, I thought, 'Lord Jesus this is different!' the following Sunday, up I went, and found there about ninety boys in the class. I just spoke simply about the Lord Jesus Christ, and at the end I said, 'If any of you chaps want to receive Jesus Christ as your Savior this afternoon, I am going to be here. Just come and talk to me afterwards.' Thirty boys came and talked to me afterwards! I hardly knew what to do with them, but I just did the best I could, and I believe God honored the desire of their hearts in spite of my clumsiness!

"Of course that was a tremendous joy to me; and this happened day after day, day after day. It did not matter what the meeting was. When I stepped out to the university that Thursday morning, I was stepping out into a new land. This was Canaan! I had had no memories of Canaan. I stepped out in blind faith. I was like the parachuter, just pulling the cord and jumping into nothing! Now I had a memory! A memory that was going to reinforce my faith for the next step into Canaan!

"So for the next meeting, I thought, 'Well, it worked last time, I wasn't quite sure that it would work, but it did; and so I will reckon upon Him again for this meeting.' I thanked the Lord again for the folk who were going to be saved, and I gave the invitation to meet me afterwards, and others were converted. When I bumped into folk on the street, I seemed always to be bumping into the right people! 'This is an extraordinary thing,' I thought. 'For seven years I was always bumping into the wrong people, and now, I can't help bumping into the right people!' For five weeks, almost every day, people were converted."

Christian friends began to notice that something was different in the life of God's young servant. He met Christians who were as weary and exhausted as he had been, and he was able to share with them the secret of the Life that vanishes depression and frustration. He and they were making the discovery that fullness of life in Christ Himself, and only in Him.

"At the end of five weeks God make it very plain to me He had something more to say. He had just begun to whet my appetite. He said, 'That is My life. You know perfectly well that it has nothing to do with you, because it happened overnight! It is not a new method. It is not a new technique that you have learned. It is simply My life; being what I *am,* doing the inevitable. This is now the thing you have got to realize; you cannot have My life for *your* program. You can only have My life for My program! That is the next issue you have got to face. In my program you are not going to be a doctor, and you are not going to Africa as a missionary. I am not complaining, that plan was sincerely conceived;' but, God made this quite plain to me. He was very kind. 'You are going to leave the university now,' He said. 'This is such a precious truth that you have that I am going to send you up and down throughout the British Isles to tell folk about it. There are lots of hungry folk, just like you were amongst the Christians, and waiting to be "bumped into" are lots of unconverted folk.'"

Thus step by step the Most High led His trusting and obedient servant into paths that he did not foresee nor choose, but they were pathways of service eminently satisfying and always adventurous. Instead of medical school and the mission field, the ministry was evangelism throughout Britain, especially among young people. Before World War II broke out he had six wonderful years of ever-expanding ministry in sharing the secret of the Life that is Christ. Major Thomas testifies: "It was just *His* victory. It was just what *He* was. I found that the simpler I could make it, the more blessing He gave; and whenever I tried to be complicated or clever, He just closed down. Only as I related situations to Him, did I find that He undertook. As soon as I related a situation to myself, He retired into the background. So I soon learned to count upon Him, because then things happened! That is the secret; it is so simple! Just to relate everything to the Lord Jesus, and take our hands off—to stand back and say, 'I thank Thee, Lord, this is Thy situation!'"

Such a course is not *inactivity,* as the Major explained, it is simply *Christ-activity.* "I found that it is anything but inactivity," he continued. "Since the war alone I have travelled a quarter of a million miles, forty-five thousand this year. I shall only be home four months out of the twelve this year, and I have got a wife and kiddies whom I love. It has been my joy to preach in Norway, and Denmark, in Germany, Austria, Switzerland, the United States and Canada, apart from the British Isles, during the past twelve months. It is not inactivity, it is simply His activity, and that is what makes the difference. It is possible to do ten times as much work as most people can do without breaking down when it is not our activity but His! Most folk break down simply because they are carrying all their own burdens and all their own problems, sleeping with them crowding in on their minds; nervous strain comes from assuming a responsibility for things that was never intended to be carried by you. Rest in Him! It is a wonderful rest. I can work through the night two or three times a week (when it is necessary sometimes I have to, though it is not to be recommended) and still feel fresher than many other folk, so long as it is His activity."

Rest of heart in the midst of activity, such is the life of adventure with the Savior. Our realization of that life is dependent wholly on our drawing on the infinite resources that are in the Savior. To young hearts at Wheaton, as well as to others, Major Thomas has given the earnest invitation: "It is all in Christ, you see; and all of Christ is yours! You can know that God has a precise place for you, which is the perfect place in His perfect plan. If never before, commit yourself totally to Him, and say, 'Lord Jesus what a wonderful thing that Thou dost know precisely what Thou dost want to do through me. Thou hast all the beautiful threads all ready to weave into the program and pattern of things. Now I am Thine! I do not want any other program, any other kind of life, but the one that Thou Thyself art prepared to live in and through me! I know, now, that all is well for me, for time and eternity.'"

That committal can open the door for you to the life of adventure with God!

A Personal Epilogue

True companionship is one of life's sweetest realities.

A companion is one who is closer than a friend or an associate. At its root the word *companion* implies the sharing of one's bread with another; thus signifying the unselfish, unreserved sharing of life and livelihood, each for the welfare of the other.

Said the Lord Jesus, "Lo, I am with you all the days, even unto the end of the age"! To realize His presence with us on life's pathway, to know that He shares our joys and our sorrows, and to be confident that He is able to supply all of our need, creates a quietness and confidence of spirit that are indispensable for the Spirit-filled life.

The life of companionship with the Lord Jesus was taught to me in many ways, but especially as a result of three crises. The first awareness of His presence came quite early in my Christian experience, during my soldiering days in World War I. Following the Armistice of November 11, 1918, my outfit, the First Division, and other American units moved eastward across the remainder of France, through Luxembourg and Belgium, into the Rhineland of Germany. Those were days of long marches in rain, mud, and snow. The wagon trains could not keep pace with the infantry, and food supplies ran short.

By the time we crossed the Rhine River into the rugged hills of Westphalia to set up the Coplanz bridgehead, I was utterly exhausted and ill. We finally reached our destination, and were billeted in a ramshackle, unheated building that had housed Russian prisoners. The weather turned bitterly cold, the snow was deep; and miserable as our quarters were, we were glad to return to them at the end of each day's maneuvers—forced marches, at least for a time, were over.

But one noon, just before Christmas, a runner from battalion headquarters came with a request to the First Sergeant that he transfer five men at once to C Company. We were with B Company of the 28th Infantry. None of us knew where C Company was located, and no one wanted to find out. I tried to be inconspicuous; but the sergeant was as contrary as all are who carry three chevrons on their sleeves, for he barked out: "Edman, you're in charge of this detail!" Four men were assigned to me, and the orders were to go at once.

While the others began to roll their few belongings into their packs, I slipped into an adjacent room, just a tiny little place that had been a sort of tavern when used by the Russians. There alone I knelt by one of the benches to pray, saying: "Lord, I cannot go. I am so ill, so worn, with such a sore throat and fever that I cannot go. And I do not know how far away C Company may be stationed!"

Then for the first time in my Christian life, as a young believer in the Lord Jesus, I was aware of a Presence beside me; nothing I could see with outer eye or touch with hand, and yet I knew He was there and that He said to me, "I will go with you."

I arose and with the strength and indefinable calmness that had come from that Presence, I shouldered my pack, took my little detail, got my directions to C Company from the Sergeant Major at battalion headquarters, and all that afternoon we trudged onward through deep snow. By nightfall we were in the village of Boden, and billeted in a home, not a prison barracks. The good mother in the home noticed that I was ill and insisted that I sleep in a feather bed upstairs rather than in the unheated room assigned to us soldiers. A feather bed, and a mother's care, and most of all the inward assurance that the Lord Jesus by His Spirit was with me!

The second major crisis came five years later. By then college days had been completed and, with my bride, delightful missionary service in the high Andes of Ecuador had begun. We had been married a little over a year when I was stricken with typhus fever, and given up to die.

I knew I was dying.

How can a person know that he is dying? He has never felt that way before, nor has anyone from the point-of-no-return come back to tell of his experience. Nevertheless, I *knew* I was dying.

I was entirely unaware of the immediate. I did not remember that a few days before I had been in little aboriginal villages in the high Ecuadorean Andes helping the children of the Incas who were dying of some mysterious malady. I did not recall the long and painful trip on horseback down mountain trails to our home in Riobamba, nor the onset of typhus fever, nor the periods of delirium, nor my being found by a fellow American who got some Indians to carry me to the railroad, nor the all-day trip to Guayaquil in a baggage car.

I did not know that my wife had been advised to prepare for the funeral and with the help of a friend had dyed black the wedding dress she had used a year before; nor that her hosts, the Will Reeds, on advice of the physician, Dr. Parker, had purchased a coffin and arranged for a brief service at three o-clock that afternoon (since, in the tropics, burial must be made soon after death).

I did recall what my mother had told me when I was a lad. Not infrequently, when people come to die, she said, in the last few moments before they slip out into eternity they experience a complete, detailed review of their life.

That happened to me.

With no effort on my part, nor any thought for that matter, I remembered the old homestead in Illinois and childhood playmates before school days began; Miss Grace, the first-grade teacher in McKinley School, and the other grades in succession; high school friends and scenes; soldiering days overseas.

How did these memories crowd in on me so clearly and accurately? That I do not know; but they did. It was something like the unfolding of a newsreel, and with it there came the clear consciousness, "Now I have come to die."

As the flashback from memory's chamber faded I felt all alone in a vast world. If there were other human beings in that quiet little hospital room, I was not conscious of them. I was utterly alone and acutely aware that in the next instant or two I would be in eternity.

Then it was that I began to be cognizant of something strangely arresting in that place—an atmosphere, an influence, a Presence. It seemed to be on the floor but it covered the area of the room, and was slowly rising to the level of the bed. I could not turn my head to see if it was real or only imaginary; but I was sure it was now reaching me. In just another moment it began to surround me, to engulf and to cover me.

Then I knew what it was, for in those moments I experienced a sweet sense of the love of God in Christ such as I had never known before in all the years of my life. So overwhelming and stupendous was that love that the Life Beyond became ineffably beautiful and infinitely better than any possible condition in this present existence. There followed moments of such sacred, intimate fellowship with Him that it is impossible to attempt to retell it. It is sufficient to say that I have no fear of dying. Heaven is home to the believer, to that one who has become a child of God through faith in the Lord Jesus Christ.

After the day when I waded so far out into the River of Death that I was closer to the other side than to this, there were about two weeks of which I have no recollection and can give no account. As I began to be conscious of being in the Parker Clinic, of the Ecuadorean nurses who cared for me, of my wife and the eight-week-old son who had come into our home, then it was that I was told the story back of my story.

Near Attleboro, Massachusetts, a rather small group had gathered in a Bible conference. In the course of their morning study they were interrupted by the conference director, Rev. E. Joseph Evans of Newton, Massachusetts, who told of a deepening burden of concern that had come upon him for the missionary in Ecuador, and he requested that they share the prayer burden with him. It was during those hours that, unknown to them, Mrs. Edman had dyed her wedding dress black, and Mr. Reed had bought a native coffin for me.

Since then I have met friends in New England who were present at that meeting. They have told me that if they should live to be a hundred years old they could never forget their kneeling to pray and their agony of spirit in their intercession for me. In the urgency of their petitions they forgot the lunch hour; but by the middle of the afternoon they experienced, they said, a lifting of spirit with the quiet assurance from heaven that their prayers for the desperate need thirty-five hundred miles away had been answered.

The deepest crisis of comradeship with Christ came to me one August morning of 1928. With Charles, the first of our four lads, then just a little fellow of three, I was onboard a little Dutch freighter, the *Boskoop,* plowing the placid Pacific toward the Gulf of Panama, bound for New York City.

I was deeply perplexed. I did not question my call to the mission field, nor did I question the five happy years that had been spent in Ecuador. As far as I knew, I was completely set apart and ready for whatever service to which I might be assigned. Compassionately I longed for the little Bible school that had been in existence just one year. Its few students were wonderfully dear to me.

As I looked back over the years, I deeply appreciated the over-shadowing of God's hand in the time debilitating illness. My life had been brought into the valley of the shadow of death, but His mercies had not failed. His compassions had been new each morning. True, my bodily strength had been greatly weakened by this prolonged and painful disease, but I looked forward to the time of returning to Ecuador when the new school term began. Surely a few months in the vigorous northern climate would restore normal health and provide a full reservoir of strength! My wife and the next little fellow, Roland, just one and one half years of age, remained in the tropics to await our return.

During the voyage my physical condition kept me confined to the stateroom, except for brief occasions. But I wasn't idle; there was much to be done. There were lessons on the life and letters of Paul to be prepared for my classes. As I worked, around me on my bunk were scattered several versions of the New Testament in Spanish and English.

I was outlining 2 Corinthians and had reached the second chapter. I came to the second paragraph, beginning at verse 12, in the American version of 1901. It read, "Now thanks be unto God which always leadeth us in triumph in Christ. . . ." The words staggered me: *always leadeth us in triumph in Christ.*

I read them over several times, slowly, thoughtfully, a word at a time. Then I turned to another translation. It read: "Wherever I go, thank God, he makes my life a constant pageant of triumph in Christ. . . ."

The contrast between this verse and my life was complete: my way seemed impenetrably obscure. Possibly a door was closing before me. Physical strength was ebbing away so that life itself might soon be done. Yet to Paul, life was "a constant pageant of triumph in Christ"! My heart therefore went out to prayer. "Dear Lord, be pleased to make my life that constant pageant of triumph, always to be led in triumph in Thee!"

The answer to that prayer was startling. By the still, small voice of the Holy Spirit there came the question, "Are you willing to go *anywhere* for Me?"

"Anywhere?"

Possibly, I thought, the Lord of the Harvest was asking me to relinquish the new little Bible school and go to some unreached area in Ecuador. After a moment or two I said slowly, "Yes, Lord, anywhere in Ecuador Thou mayest say."

"I did not say 'in Ecuador,'" came the answer, "I said, '*Anywhere.*'"

Not necessarily in Ecuador? Possibly not in Latin America? Even possibly not on the mission field? Just *anywhere* at all? The questions tumbled over themselves in my mind. For a long time I looked across the wide wastes of the Pacific, conscious that the Lord Himself stood by my side, awaiting the answer.

Then quietly, with utter sincerity, came the choice: "Yes, Lord, anywhere Thou sayest I will go, only that my life may be always a constant pageant of triumph in Thee."

During those sacred moments in the crisis of comradeship I had utterly abandoned myself to Him. Who would not do anything, go anywhere, be anything He decreed, He, the unspeakably precious companion? Could any choice be as wonderful as His will? Could any place be safer than the center of His will? Did not He assure me by His very presence that His thoughts toward us are good, and not evil?

Death to my own plans and desires was almost deliriously delightful. Everything was laid at His nail-scarred feet, life or death, health or illness, appreciation by others or misunderstanding, success or failure as measured by human standards. Only He Himself mattered.

I remembered the testimony of George Müller when he told of the moment when he died to self, to ambition, to the praise or blame of men, only that he might live in Christ.

How long my heart stood in His presence I don't know. The decision had been made. There was yieldedness for any door, however large or small it might seem, or for no door at all. I was confident that the Faithful One was able to do "exceeding abundantly above all that we ask or think, according to the power that worketh in us." There could be no self-confidence, no cockiness of spirit, no contempt for any path in which He might lead or for any cross that He might give.

After the inexpressibly sweet communion with the Savior and the choice of utter abandonment, something else came. It was the commission: *Anywhere!* With that command there was granted the confidence: *Always leadeth in triumph in Christ—a constant pageant of triumph in Christ!*

Soon afterward I received a quiet and gracious corroboration of the divine commission. One of our younger Ecuadorean Christians had backslidden. Leaving his native land, he had gone to New York City. I had no address nor the faintest knowledge of his whereabouts. All I had was a deep prayer, "Lord, I would like to see Gonzalo and bring him back to Thee." But how could I find him among the millions of New York City? I was practically an invalid and having arrived in the city I had to remain in bed at the missionary home.

Several evenings after we landed, as Charles and I were having our devotions before retiring, there came a knock on the door—and in walked Gonzalo! We embraced in the Latin American way and shared our tears, and an hour later he was led back into fellowship with the Lord.

Always leadeth in triumph—if anywhere!

Life with this divine companion becomes an adventure. My health gradually returned, and there came a call to minister in a little church at the edge of Worcester, Massachusetts. The word from the Lord was quiet yet challenging: "Fear not, O land; be glad and rejoice: for the LORD will do great things" (Joel 2:21). For some time I saw no fulfillment of that promise; but one day the Lord of the harvest opened the door at radio station WORC for a morning watch program. Then, too, for good measure, the Lord allowed me to take graduate work at Clark University until I received a Ph.D. in the field of International Relations.

In the early hours of a January morning in 1936, when outside all was blackness and bitter cold, the Lord spoke to me quietly, "Wheaton College." I had never thought of that. Inwardly I was reluctant to consider it unless it should be most clearly the command from heaven. Therefore, the matter was left committed to the Lord. Two months later confirmation came, wholly unsolicited, of course, in an invitation from Wheaton to become a member of its faculty.

In the "pageant of triumph" the promise of Numbers 9:20 had become a wonderful reality: "And so it was, when the cloud was a few days upon the tabernacle; according to the commandment of the LORD they abode in their tents, and according to the commandment of the LORD they journeyed."

Divine comradeship has made many other promises personal and sweet. Among them are Jeremiah 29:11—"For I know the thoughts that I think toward you, saith the LORD, thoughts of peace, and not of evil, to give you an expected end." Also John 10:4 is a constant assurance: "And when he putteth forth his own sheep, he goeth before them, and the sheep follow him: for they know his voice." Especially strong under all circumstances is Nahum 1:7 which has become something of a life text to me: "The LORD is good, a strong hold in the day of trouble; and he knoweth them that trust in him."

These are some of the consequences of the choice to accept His commission "Anywhere," and to trust Him for victory. Into this adventure of faith God has brought many friends: His Majesty Haile Selassie in Ethopia and Her Excellency Madame Chiang Kai-shek in Free China; Christian businessmen like Robert G. LeTourneau of Texas and Kenneth S. Keyes of Florida; a soldier like General William K. Harrison and a missionary statesman like Cameron Townsend. Fellow pilgrims on this shining pathway have included Wheaton students like Ruth and Billy Graham, also Ed McCully, Jim Elliot and Nate Saint martyred in Ecuador.

Ethiopia and Macedonia, Sweden and Switzerland, Jordan and Israel, Liberia and Peru, Korea, Formosa, Japan, Hong Kong and Australia are some of the spheres of challenging service to which the Lord has directed me in these busy and happy days while at Wheaton.

There is continuance of the command: *Anywhere,* with the confidence of *always.* Frequently the same question comes: "Are you willing to go *anywhere* that I say, at any time?"

The answer is yet the same; and please God, always will be: "Yes, Lord, anywhere, at any time, so that life will be indeed this constant pageant of triumph in Thee."

Anywhere . . . always!

The life of companionship by the Holy Spirit is indeed "the path of the just [which] is as the shining light, that shineth more and more unto the perfect day"!

Conclusion

The life that wins is an actuality, not just an aspiration.

Its secret is simple, and yet profound. It is plain to the heart filled with faith and obedience, but it is perplexing to self-will and self-effort. It is an obtainment, not an attainment; a gift to be received and not an achievement to be earned. It is from above and not from within ourselves; it is from heaven and is revealed on earth. Its life arises out of death to ourselves and not from deeds that we have done.

The details in individual experience differ appreciably, and are related to the personality and the circumstances of that life. Beyond the details, however, the pattern of the exchanged life is quite the same for each one. First, there is an *awareness* of our need, as expressed by the Lord Jesus, "If any man thirst . . ." (John 7:37). In similar vein the psalmist prayed: ". . . my soul thirsteth for thee, my flesh longeth for thee in a dry and thirsty land, where no water is; To see thy power and thy glory . . ." (Ps. 63:1, 2).

Then there is *agony* of soul because of that awareness. One remembers the beatitude: "Blessed are they which do hunger and thirst after righteousness: for they shall be filled" (Matt. 5:6). Hunger and thirst are not happy experiences, but they lead to true happiness. Crucifixion is a most painful process and the soul that longs for fullness of life in Christ finds that the doorway to it is death to self. The Scriptures declare plainly: "They that are Christ's have crucified the flesh with the affections and lusts" (Gal. 5:24). It may seem that agony of soul is beyond endurance, but beyond it one comes to the glorious realization described in Galatians 2:20—"I am crucified with Christ: nevertheless I live; yet not I, but Christ liveth I me: and the life which I now live in the flesh I live by the faith of the Son of God, who loved me, and gave himself for me."

Then follows wholehearted, unreserved *abandonment* to the Savior. Sick of self and sin we obey the clear injunction of Romans 6:13: ". . . yield yourselves unto God, as those that are alive from the dead, and your members as instruments of righteousness unto God." Thereby Romans 12:1, 2 becomes a living word to us: "I beseech you therefore, brethren, by the mercies of God, that ye present your bodies a living sacrifice, holy, acceptable unto God, which is your reasonable service. And be not conformed to this world: but be ye transformed by the renewing of your mind, that ye may prove what is that good, and acceptable, and perfect, will of God."

Life, however, is not achieved by longing for a better life and lingering at the cross. There must be *appropriation* by faith of the Holy Spirit to fill life with the presence of the Lord Jesus. That obtainment is by faith, and not by works. Inquires the Scripture: "This only would I learn of you, Received ye the Spirit by the works of the law, or by the hearing of faith?" (Gal. 3:2). Just as salvation is by faith, so also is the exchanged life. Just as we accept the Lord Jesus by faith as Savior, so by simple faith we receive the fullness of the Holy Spirit. Just as we took the Lord as our sin-bearer, we take the Holy Spirit as our burden-bearer. Just as we take the Savior as our penalty for sins that are past, we take the Holy Spirit for power over indwelling sins that are present. The Savior is our atonement, the Holy Spirit is our advocate. In salvation we receive newness of life, by the Holy Spirit we find life more abundant. In each case the appropriation is by faith, and by faith alone, wholly apart from any feeling on our part.

Following appropriation there is *abiding* by faith in the Savior. Did He not say: "Abide in me, and I in you. As the branch cannot bear fruit of itself, except it abide in the vine; no more can ye, except ye abide in me. I am the vine, ye are the branches: He that abideth in me, and I in him, the same bringeth forth much fruit: for without me ye can do nothing" (John 15:4–5)? Abiding is obedience to His will. Declares 1 John 3:24: "And he that keepeth his commandments dwelleth in him, and he in him. And hereby we know that he abideth in us, by the Spirit which he hath given us." Abiding is not striving nor struggling, learned Hudson Taylor, but a resting in the Faithful One, and implicit obedience to Him. The surrendered life that abides is a life of surrender.

The exchanged life is one of *abundance.* The Savior promised "rivers of living water" to flow from the Spirit-filled life (John 7:38). There is provision for life more abundant (John 10:10). And that life is indeed one of constant *adventure,* for it learns the wonderful reality of John 10:4: "And when he putteth forth his own sheep, he goeth before them, and the sheep follow him: for they know his voice." Who knows where He will lead and what He will say? Ear is tender to hear His voice, and heart is on tiptoe to see what next the Altogether Lovely One will do.

And that life can be yours and mine!

Bibliography

Baird, John. *The Spiritual Unfolding of Bishop H. C. G. Moule* (London: Oliphants, Ltd.), 1926.

Barabas, Steven. *So Great Salvation: The History and Message of the Keswick Convention* (London: Marshall, Morgan and Scott), 1952.

Brengle, S. L. *When the Holy Ghost Is Come,* 5th ed. (New York: The Salvation Army Printing and Publishing House), 1926.

Bunyan, John. *Grace Abounding to the Chief of Sinners,* Vol. VIII of *Practical Works* (Philadelphia: American Baptist Publishing Society), 1852.

_____. *The Holy War* (Philadelphia: Presbyterian Board of Publications), 1803.

_____. *Pilgrim's Progress* (Cincinnati: United States Book and Bible Company), 1879.

Carmichael, Amy. *Beginning of a Story* (London: Society for Promoting Christian Knowledge), 1908.

_____. *Continuation of a Story* (London: Society for Promoting Christian Knowledge), 1909.

_____. *Gold Cord* (London: Society for Promoting Christian Knowledge), 1932.

_____. *Kohila* (London: Society for Promoting Christian Knowledge), 1938.

_____. *Meal in a Barrel* (London: Society for Promoting Christian Knowledge), 1928.

_____. *Ploughed Under* (London: Society for Promoting Christian Knowledge), 1934.

_____. *Things As They Are* (London: Society for Promoting Christian Knowledge), 1901.

_____. *Though the Mountains Shake* (New York: Loizeaux Brothers), 1946.

_____. *Toward Jerusalem* (London: Society for Promoting Christian Knowledge), 1936.

_____. *Windows* (London: Society for Promoting Christian Knowledge), 1937.

Douglas, W. M. *Andrew Murray and His Message* (London: Oliphants, Ltd.), n.d.

Duplessis, Johannes. *The Life of Andrew Murray of South Africa* (London: Marshall Brothers, Ltd.), 1919.

Edman, V. Raymond. *Finney Lives On* (New York: Fleming H. Revell Company), 1951.

Farwell, John W. *Early Recollections of Dwight L. Moody* (Chicago: Bible Institute Colportage Association), n.d.

Gordon, Adoniram Judson. *How Christ Came to Church,* with the life story by A. T. Pierson (Philadelphia: American Baptist Publication Society), 1896.

_____. *In Christ; or, The Believer's Union with His Lord* (New York: Fleming H. Revell Company), 1880.

_____. *Ministry of the Spirit* (Philadelphia: American Baptist Publication Society), 1894.

_____. *The Twofold Life; or Christ's Work for Us and Christ's Work in Us* (New York: Fleming H. Revell Company), 1883.

Gordon, Ernest. *Adoniram Judson Gordon** (New York: Fleming H. Revell), 1896.

Hall, Clarence W. *Samuel Logan Brengle: Portrait of a Prophet* (New York: the National Headquarters, The Salvation Army, Inc.), 1933.

Harford, John Batterby and Macdonald, Frederick Charles. *Handley Carr Glyn Moule, Bishop of Durham: A Biography,* 2nd ed. (London: Hodder and Stoughton), 1922.

Havergal, Frances Ridley. *Poems* (New York: E. P. Dutton and Company), 1885.

Havergal, Maria V. G. *Memorials of Frances Ridley Havergal by Her Sister* (New York: Anson D. R. Randolph and Company), 1880.

Houghton, Frank. *Amy Carmichael of Dohnavur* (London: Society for Promoting Christian Knowledge), 1953.

---

*A biography with letters and illustrative extracts drawn from unpublished or uncollected sermons and addresses, by his son.

Howard, Philip Eugene. *Charles Gallaudet Trumbull: Apostle of the Victorious Life* (Philadelphia: The Sunday School Times Company), 1944.

McGaw, Francis A. *Praying Hyde* (Chicago: Moody Press), 1930.

Miller, Basil. *Praying Hyde: A Man of Prayer* (Grand Rapids: Zondervan), 1943.

Moody, D. L. *Glad Tidings, Comprising Sermons and Prayer-meeting Talks Delivered at the New York Hippodrome* (New York: E. B. Trent), 1876.

Moody, William R. *The Life of Dwight L. Moody* (New York: Fleming H. Revell Company), 1900.

Moule, Handley C. G. *Christ Is All* (London: Hodder and Stoughton), n.d.

_____. *The Old Gospel for the New Age* (New York: Fleming H. Revell company), 1901

Murray, Andrew. *Abide in Christ, Thoughts on the Blessed Life of Fellowship with the Son of God* (Chicago: Fleming H. Revell), n.d.

_____. *Absolute Surrender* (London: Marshall Brothers, Ltd.), 1932.

_____. *The Holiest of All: An Exposition of the Epistle of the Hebrews* (London: James Nisbet and Company), 1896.

_____. *Like Christ* (New York: American Tract Society), n.d.

_____. *The Master's Indwelling* (Chicago: Fleming H. Revell Company), 1896.

_____. *With Christ in the School of Prayer: Thoughts on our Training for the Ministry of Intercession* (Chicago: Fleming H. Revell Company), 1885.

Price, Eugenia. *The Burden Is Light!* (Westwood, N.J.: Fleming H. Revell Company), 1955.

_____. *Discoveries, Made from Living My New Life* (Grand Rapids: Zondervan), 1953.

_____. *Early Will I Seek Thee* (Westwood, N.J.: Fleming H. Revell), 1956.

_____. *Never a Dull Moment* (Grand Rapids: Zondervan), 1955.

Smith, Wilbur M. *Dwight Lyman Moody: An Annotated Bibliography* (Chicago: Moody Press), 1948.

Taylor, Dr. and Mrs. Howard. *Hudson Taylor's Spiritual Secret* (London, Philadelphia: China Inland Mission), 1932.

Taylor, Mrs. Howard. *Story of China Inland Mission* (London: Morgan), 1894.

Trumbull, Charles G. *The Life That Wins* (Philadelphia: The Sunday School Times Company), n.d.

_____. *Taking Men Alive: Studies in the Principles and Practice of Individual Soul-winning* (New York: Association Press), 1916.

Wilson, Walter Lewis. *Let's Go Fishing with the Doctor* (Findlay, Ohio: Fundamental Truth Publishers), 1932.

_____. *Ye Know Him: or What Is the Holy Spirit to You?* (Grand Rapids: Zondervan), 1949.